A TASTE OF TOFU

Mastering The Art of Tofu Cooking

PUBLISHER REPRESENTATIVE OFFICE
UNITED STATES: Prime Communication System
P.O.BOX456 Shaw Island, WA 98286
AUTHOR'S SALES AGENCY: A.K. HARANO COMPANY
P.O. Box 1005 Cypress, CA 90630
Phone: (714) 739-2755
D & BH ENTERPRISES
94-443 Kahuanani Street, Waipahu, HI 96797
Phone: (808) 671-6041

OVERSEAS DISTRIBUTORS
UNITED STATES: JP TRADING, INC.
300 Industrial Way
Brisbane, Calif. 94005
Phone: (415) 468-0775, 0776
MEXICO: Publicaciones Sayrols, S.A. de C.V.
COLOMBIA: Jorge E. Morales & CIA. LTDA.
TAIWAN: Formosan Magazine Press, Ltd.
HONG KONG: Apollo Book Company, Ltd.
THAILAND: Central Department Store Ltd.
SINGAPORE: MPH DISTRIBUTORS (S) PTE, LTD.
MALAYSIA: MPH DISTRIBUTORS SDN, BHD.
PHILIPPINES: National Book Store, Inc.
KOREA: Tongjin Chulpan Muyeok Co., Ltd.
INDONESIA: C.V. TOKO BUKU "MENTENG"
INDIA: Dani Book Land, Bombay 14
AUSTRALIA: BOOKWISE INTERNATIONAL
GUAM, SIPAN AND MICRONESIAN ISLANDS: ISLAND PLANT-LIFE PRODUCTS

ISBN4-915249-46-8

CONTENTS

PREFACE

To the best of my belief, proper nutrition and common sense living are man's best medicine. I grew up knowing that my mother was a gifted cook who communicated to me her knowledges about good foods and nutrition. We spent many years cooking together. I was fortunate to realize then that not only learning about just cooking but also learning about good nutrition was important. Ever since I started teaching cooking on the West Coast of the United States, there have been many friends who wanted to learn more about Asian cooking which eventually led me to write cook books. I am under the impression that, since I wrote my first TOFU COOK BOOK in 1982, many more people have become aware of the importance of good nutrition to health, and have opened their eyes to the wonderfully nutritional, yet inexpensive soybean products. Statistics show that the average Americans spend 96 cents (or more) of every health dollars on treatment of disease and injuries, and only 4 cents (or less) of every dollar on prevention. I have tried to introduce nutritionally valued *tofu* to people who have not yet eaten and / or are willing to expand their *tofu* recipes. The *tofu* book provides simple and easy ways to approach *tofu* cooking and helps to know texture and flavor. All recipes appearing in the book use fresh *tofu* which is readily available at food markets.

Many of you are already familiar with *tofu* and other soybean products. Included in this book are recipes not only for *tofu* cooking but for other *tofu* products such as deep-fried *tofu* pouches (ABURA AGE), deep-fried *tofu* cutlets (ATSU AGE), deep-fried *tofu* burgers (GANMODOKI), grilled *tofu* (YAKI DOFU), freeze-dried *tofu* (KOYA DOFU), dried bean curd sheets (YUBA) and soy pulp (OKARA).

The ingredients are available at most of Oriental markets, some health food stores and supermarkets. *Tofu* and *tofu* products can add to the nutritional value of your menu in the form of exciting but inexpensive new dishes. Please note, however, for one thing I'm not writing this book to put you on a diet or for medical treatment. My intent in this book is to introduce to you tasty and attractive *tofu* and other *tofu* products, which can be cooked quick and easy. *Tofu* is remarkably versatile. Please experiment, be inventive and ingenious, and enjoy the fascinating cooking. Some of the ingredients in the recipes may be unfamiliar to you. The ingredients are listed on page 98 describing in details.

I hope this book will be welcomed by nutrition-conscious people as well as gourmet cooks.

Tokyo, Japan
January, 1988

Yukiko Moriyama

ACKNOWLEDGMENTS

I would like to express my heartfelt gratitude to SHIRO SHIMURA, publisher of JOIE, INC., and his wonderful staff for their trust and faith in my work.

Also I would like to give special thanks to the following individuals for their support, encouragement and patience throughout many months of compiling the materials in this book:

RYOJI SONODA, TSUGUHIRO SATO: Design
YASUHIRO KOMATSU: Food photographs
AKIRA NAITO, FUKI KASUGAI: Editorial assistance
MICHIKO HAYASHI, MARIKO SUZUKI: Illustrations
IKUKO KOBAYASHI, EIKO OISHI: Kitchen help

INTRODUCTION

Soybeans are perhaps the world's oldest crop, and for centuries, they have meant meat, milk, cheese, bread and oil to the peoples in the Orient. In fact, TOFU (bean curd), firm yogurt, cottage cheese, or cheese-like pure white loaf made from the curds of soybean milk is called cheese in the Orient.

Soybean products have played a dominant role in Asian cooking for centuries, but the Western Hemisphere knows of soybeans too little since Westerners have not had to use them as a food. However, more than two hundred commercial products are made from soybeans. In recent years, soybean products came into the limelight of our diet for their nutritional merits. *Tofu*, soy sauce and *miso* are perhaps the best known products to the Western world. The protein content in soybeans is much higher than that of other foods. For instance, two pounds of soy flour are equal in protein content to five pounds of boneless meat, six dozen eggs, fifteen quarts of milk or four pounds of cheese. Therefore, soybeans should not be considered primarily as just a meat substitute but rather as a protein food that can fortify other foods.

Tofu is the most fascinating product of all soybean foods. It is a white, tasteless cake, perhaps most unusual to many. *Tofu* is very easily digestible for everyone. Study on soy protein digestion rate was made by the Japanese Scientific Research Council recently. It is said that cooked soybeans and fermented soybeans, *natto* in Japanese, 90% and *tofu*, soymilk, protein powder and other processed soybean products 95% digest. Soybeans contain protein, linoleic acid, lecithin, vitamins B & E, calcium and other essential nutrients. *Tofu* is low in saturated fats, low in carbohydrates, low in calories and entirely free of cholesterol. The data presented on page 101 shows nutrients in *tofu* of various types.

Fresh *tofu* is sold at the produce section or the refrigerated foods section of many supermarkets, health food stores and Oriental groceries. Weights vary somewhere between $10\frac{1}{2}$ and 20 ounces (300 and 570 grams). A fairly recent addition to the market is powder to make your own *tofu* and *tofu* packed in a carton which can be preserved at room temperatures up to six months. Canned *tofu* and dried-frozen *tofu* are also available. Deep-fried *tofu* pouches are sometimes found in the frozen food compartments. Canned deep-fried *tofu* pouches are also available, though some are already seasoned.

I wrote the recipes in detail and showed as many step-by-step process pictures as possible in this book, so that anyone unfamiliar with *tofu* cooking can follow them and feel confident of good results.

Almost all the recipes, except a few, serve four. These amounts allow flexibility and can be halved or doubled successfully. The technique, for example, of draining *tofu* before cooking may seem unnecessarily fussy, but it does produce a better taste as *tofu* contains lots of water. You will find *tofu* preparation tips on page 91.

Buying some cooking equipment is very worthwhile, such as a wok and a bamboo steamer, although any reasonably well-equipped kitchens may have all that is needed. Most of the recipes take only a short time to prepare and are easy to cook.

It is precisely this kind of home cooking that I would like to share with you.

BASIC COOKING INFORMATION

1 cup is equivalent to 240 ml in our recipes: (American cup measurement)
1 American cup = 240 ml = 8 American fl oz
1 British cup = 200 ml = 7 British fl oz
1 Japanese cup = 200 ml

1 tablespoon = 15 ml   1 teaspoon = 5 ml

ABBREVIATIONS USED IN THIS BOOK

C = cup (s)	T = tablespoon (s)	t = teaspoon (s)	fl = fluid	oz = ounce (s)
lb (s) = pound (s)	ml = mililiter	g = grams	in = inch (es)	cm = centimeter
F = Fahrenheit	C = Celsius	doz = dozen	pkg (s) = package (s)	
pt (s) = pint (s)	qt (s) = quart(s)			

TABLES CONVERTING FROM U.S. CUSTOMARY SYSTEM TO METRICS

Liquid Measures

U.S. Customary system	oz	g	ml
$1/16$ cup = 1 T	$1/2$ oz	14 g	15 ml
$1/4$ cup = 4 T	2 oz	60 g	59 ml
$1/2$ cup = 8 T	4 oz	115 g	118 ml
1 cup = 16 T	8 oz	225 g	236 ml
$1 3/4$ cups	14 oz	400 g	414 ml
2 cups = 1 pint	16 oz	450 g	473 ml
3 cups	24 oz	685 g	710 ml
4 cups	32 oz	900 g	946 ml

Liquid Measures

Japanese system	oz	ml
$1/8$ cup	$7/8$ oz	25 ml
$1/4$ cup	$1 3/4$ oz	50 ml
$1/2$ cup	$3 1/2$ oz	100 ml
1 cup	7 oz	200 ml
$1 1/2$ cups	$10 1/2$ oz	300 ml
2 cups	14 oz	400 ml
3 cups	21 oz	600 ml
4 cups	28 oz	800 ml

Weights

ounces to grams*
$1/4$ oz = 7 g
$1/2$ oz = 14 g
1 oz = 30 g
2 oz = 60 g
4 oz = 115 g
6 oz = 170 g
8 oz = 225 g
16 oz = 450 g

*Equivalent

Linear Measures

inches to centimeters
$1/2$ in = 1.27 cm
1 in = 2.54 cm
2 in = 5.08 cm
4 in = 10.16 cm
5 in = 12.7 cm
10 in = 25.4 cm
15 in = 38.1 cm
20 in = 50.8 cm

Temperatures

Fahrenheit (F) to Celsius (C)		
freezer storage	−10°F =	−23.3°C
	0°F =	−17.7°C
water freezes	32°F =	0 °C
	68°F =	20 °C
	100°F =	38 °C
water boils	212°F =	100 °C
	300°F =	150 °C
	400°F =	204.4°C

Deep-Frying Oil Temperatures

300°F − 330°F (150°C − 165°C) = low
340°F − 350°F (170°C − 175°C) = moderate
350°F − 360°F (175°C − 180°C) = high

Oven Temperatures

250°F − 350°F (120°C − 175°C) = low or cool
350°F − 400°F (175°C − 204°C) = moderate or medium
400°F − 450°F (204°C − 230°C) = hot
450°F − 500°F (230°C − 260°C) = very hot

INGREDIENTS

A *TOFU* & SOYBEAN PRODUCTS

1. SOYMILK
2. SOYBEANS
3. *OKARA*
4. FERMENTED SOYBEANS (*NATTO*)
5. GRILLED *TOFU* (*YAKI-DOFU*)
6. SOFT *TOFU*
7. FIRM *TOFU*
8. BEAN CURD SHEETS (*YUBA*)
9. DEEP-FRIED *TOFU* POUCH (*ABURAAGE*)
10. DEEP-FRIED *TOFU* BURGER (*GANMODOKI*)
11. DEEP-FRIED *TOFU* CUTLET (*ATSUAGE*)
12. FROZEN *TOFU* (*KOYA-DOFU*)

B DRIED FOODS

1. GOURD STRIPS (*KANPYO*)
2. BEAN THREADS
3. DRIED BONITO FLAKES
4. CLOUD EAR MUSHROOMS
5. *SHIITAKE* MUSHROOMS
6. *NORI* SEAWEED
7. BUCKWHEAT NOODLES
8. THICK NOODLES
9. KELP (*KOMBU*)
10. *WAKAME* SEAWEED
11. GELATINE
12. SESAME SEEDS (WHITE)
13. SESAME SEEDS (BLACK)
14. SOYBEANS
15. DRIED SHRIMP
16. FROZEN *TOFU*
    (*KOYA-DOFU*)

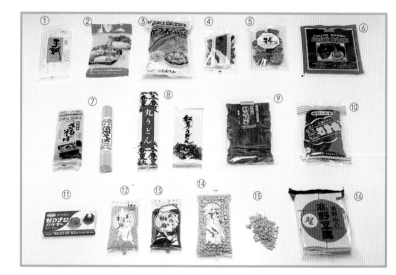

C SEASONINGS

1. *MISO*
2. CHILI OIL
3. OYSTER SAUCE
4. SWEET BEAN SAUCE
5. SESAME SEED OIL
6. *MIRIN*
7. VINEGAR
8. KETCHUP
9. SOY SAUCE
10. LOW SALT SOY SAUCE
11. LIGHT SOY SAUCE
12. HONEY
13. WORCESTERSHIRE SAUCE
14. *TONKATSU* SAUCE
15. LOW-CALORIE COOKING OIL SPRAY
16. MAYONNAISE
17. HOT BEAN PASTE
18. SWEET BEAN PASTE
19. GRATED GARLIC
20. GRATED GINGERROOT
21. *WASABI* PASTE
22. CHINESE MUSTARD PASTE
23. *SAKE*
24. *DASHI-NO-MOTO* (INSTANT *DASHI* MIX)
25. DILL WEED
26. *SANSHO* POWDER
27. 7-SPICE POWDER
28. PEPPER
29. CRUSHED RED PEPPER
30. CHICKEN SOUP STOCK
31. CHICKEN BOUILLON CUBES
32. CINNAMON
33. CURRY POWDER
34. MUSTARD POWDER
35. DRIED RED PEPPER
36. HORSERADISH MUSTARD

TOFU CHEESE BALLS

This delightful recipe makes a colorful addition to a party menu.

1¼ in (3.5 cm) diameter balls

28 oz (800 g) firm *tofu*, well drained

A ⎰ 1 t   each soy sauce, salt
     ⎱ ¼ t   pepper
        4 T   cornstarch

4 slices cheese, chopped
4 slices cooked ham, chopped
Oil for deep-frying (350°F/175°C)

Dipping sauce
⎰ 3 T   ketchup
⎱ 1 T   Worcestershire sauce

Condiments
Chinese mustard, Mayonnaise

1. Beat *tofu* and mix with ingredients **A**. Set aside. Mix chopped cheese and ham.

2. Place about 1 T of *tofu* mixture on palm of hand and flatten out with fingers.

3. Place 2 t cheese and ham mixture.

4. Cover with 1 T of *tofu* mixture. Form small ball. Repeat.

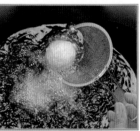

5. Heat deep frying oil to 350°F (175°C); deep fry balls until golden brown. Serve hot with dipping sauce.

TUNA BALLS

INGREDIENTS: Makes 30 balls

20–21 oz (570g–600g) *tofu*, well drained
1 6^1/$_2$ oz (185g) can tuna, drained
Some pepper
1 stalk green onion, finely chopped
^{1}/$_2$ T vegetable oil
Oil for deep-frying (350°F/ 175°C)

These tuna balls are crisp on the outside and soft in the inside.

1. Beat *tofu*.

2. Mix *tofu* with tuna, pepper and green onion.

3. Make balls, one tablespoonful each, wet palms of hands with oil for ease in handling.

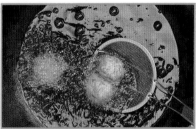

4. Heat oil in a wok, fry few pieces at a time until golden brown or 5 to 6 minutes.

NOTE: Salmon can be used instead of tuna.

11

TOFU WITH DRIED BONITO FLAKES *(Tosa-dofu)*

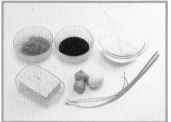

14–16 oz (400g–450g) firm
tofu, well drained
1 egg, beaten
All-purpose flour for dusting
1²/₃ C dried bonito flakes
¹/₃ C black sesame seeds
Some vegetable oil
Garnishes
Chopped green onion
Grated fresh gingerroot

1. Cut *tofu* into 1 in (2.5 cm) cubes.

2. Mix bonito flakes and sesame seeds and set aside.
3. Coat *tofu* cubes with flour, beaten egg and bonito flakes mixture.

Dried bonito flakes give extra cheese-like flavor to this very nutritious appetizer.

4. Heat 2 T oil in a skillet over medium high heat; add *tofu* and sauté until brown on both sides. Place on a platter and serve with garnishes and soy sauce.

DEEP-FRIED FERMENTED SOYBEANS *(Natto no karaage)*

This recipe is ideal for the introduction of *natto*.

2 3¹/₂ oz (100g) each *natto* package
A ⎰ 2 T   green onion, chopped
  ⎱ 2 t   Chinese mustard
    8 T   cornstarch
    1¹/₂ T soy sauce
    1 T   toasted sesame seeds (optional)
3–4 C vegetable oil for deep-frying
    (350°F/175°C)

1. Mix *natto* with ingredients **A**.

2. Heat oil in 3-quart saucepan to 350°F (175°C).
3. Drop one tablespoonful of *natto* in oil, turning occasionally, 4 to 5 minutes.
4. Drain on paper towels; sprinkle sesame seeds while hot. Serve with salt or soy sauce.

NATTO TEMPURA (*Natto no tempura*)

DEEP-FRIED FERMENTED
SOYBEANS
(See page 12)

NATTO TEMPURA

Natto is available in many large supermarkets and at Oriental grocery stores.

INGREDIENTS: 4 servings

1   3¹/₂ oz (100 g) *natto* package
A { 1 t green onion, chopped
       1 t Chinese mustard
       1 t soy sauce
2 sheets *nori* seaweed, 8¹/₄ × 7¹/₄
   in (21 × 18 cm), cut into fourths
8 *shiso* leaves or spinach leaves
Oil for deep-frying (350°F/175°C)
***Tempura* batter**
   ¹/₂ C all-purpose flour
   ¹/₂ C ice water

1. Mix *natto* with ingredients **A.**
2. Divide into eighths.

5. Mix flour and water and coat *natto* roll.

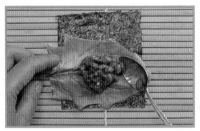

3. Place *shiso* or spinach leaf on *nori* and place *natto* on top.
4. Roll up.

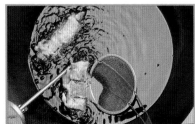

6. Deep-fry, turning occasionally, 4 to 5 minutes. Drain on paper towels. Serve hot.

TOFU WITH WAKAME SEAWEED SOUPS

CLEAR SOUP (*Suimono*)

Starting your meal with a bowl of hot, low-calorie *wakame* seaweed soup gives you a new taste treat.

MISO SOUP (*Miso-shiru*)

4–7 oz (115–200g) soft *tofu*
1³/₄ oz (50g) dried *wakame* seaweed
3¹/₄ C *dashi* stock
1 t salt
1¹/₂–2 t light soy sauce
Some *yuzu* or lemon peels

1. Cut *tofu* into ³/₈ in (1 cm) cubes.
2. Soften dried *wakame* seaweed in water; chop into small pieces. ↗

3. In 3-quart saucepan, heat *dashi* stock, salt, soy sauce, *tofu* and *wakame* seaweed over medium high heat until it boils.
4. Cook for another 30 seconds. Serve hot and sprinkle some peels.

4 oz (115g) *tofu*
1 deep-fried *tofu* pouch (*aburaage*)
1³/₄ oz (50g) dried *wakame* seaweed
3¹/₄ C *dashi* stock
3 T white *miso*

Mild white *miso* adds a distinctive flavor to this soup.

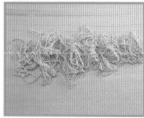

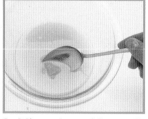

1. Cut *tofu* into ³/₈ in (1 cm) cubes.
2. Dip deep-fried *tofu* pouch into boiling water for 30 seconds to remove grease. Drain on paper towels; slice thin.

3. Soften dried *wakame* seaweed; trim hard ends and chop into small pieces.
4. In 3-quart saucepan, heat *dashi* stock over medium high heat. Add *tofu* pouch pieces; cook for a minute.

5. Mix *miso* with small amount of *dashi* stock in a small bowl; pour into saucepan.
6. Add *tofu* and *wakame* seaweed and cook until just before boiling point. Remove from heat.

NOTE: Be careful not to boil over *miso* soup as flavor will be gone by overcooking. Red *miso* can be substituted for white *miso*. Add small amount of soy sauce if you prefer richer taste.

CHINESE STYLE *TOFU* SOUP

INGREDIENTS: 8 servings

10-12 oz (285-340g) soft *tofu*
1/4 C dried shrimp
4 medium dried *shiitake* mushrooms
2 1/2 oz (70g) bamboo shoots
1/2 cucumber
1 T minced gingerroot
2 green onion
2 cans (10 3/4 oz / 310g each) condensed chicken broth
2/3 t salt, 1/8 t pepper
1 T cornstarch plus 2 T water
2 1/2 t rice vinegar
1/2 t sesame oil
1 T vegetable oil

This is a homemade version of the popular Chinese soup. This recipe makes an ideal first course for an intimate dinner party.

1. Cut *tofu* into 1/2 in (1.5 cm) cubes.

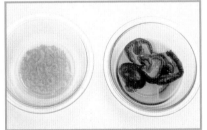

2. Soften dried shrimp and *shiitake* mushrooms in lukewarm water. Reserve soak. Trim off stem ends from mushrooms and slice thin.

3. Cut bamboo shoots into 1/2 in (1.5 cm) cubes, and slice cucumber. Cut green onion into 1 in (2.5 cm) long pieces.

4. Heat 1 T oil in wok; add gingerroot and green onion. Stir fry over high heat for 1 minute.

5. Add shrimp, *shiitake* mushrooms, bamboo shoots and cucumber; stir fry for 2 to 3 minutes.

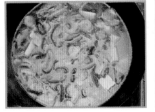

6. Add chicken broth and 2 cans water, and *shiitake* soaking liquid and bring to a boil. Skim scums. Add *tofu*, salt and pepper.

7. Thicken with cornstarch mixture. Add rice vinegar and sesame oil; stir. Remove from heat.

TOFU AND FERMENTED SOYBEAN SOUP *(Natto-jiru)*

Served in a large bowl with steamed hot rice and salad. It makes a nutritious yet delicious vegetarian soup supper.

INGREDIENTS: 4 servings

1 3$^1/_2$ oz (100 g) *natto* package
$^1/_2$ – 1 cake of *konnyaku* (devil's tongue) sliced into thin strips
14 oz (400 g) firm *tofu*
2 C chopped *mitsuba* trefoil or green vegetable leaves
3$^1/_4$ C *dashi* stock
3 level T red *miso*
Chopped green onion (optional)

1. Cut *tofu* into 1 in (2.5 cm) cubes.

2. Chop, mash or grind *natto* and mix with small amount of *dashi* stock.

3. In 3-quart saucepan, heat *dashi* stock and add *konnyaku* strips; bring to a boil. Add red *miso, natto* and *tofu*; stir to mix and cook for 1 to 2 minutes over medium high heat until almost boiling. Add chopped *mitsuba* and remove from heat. Sprinkle with chopped green onion.

NOTE: Deep-fried *tofu* pouches, taro, *shiitake* mushrooms or green onion can be added to this soup.

16

This slow cooking casserole is an all time favorite of the Japanese. It can be served at an intimate party on a table giving each person easy access to all of the ingredients in the hot pot.

INGREDIENTS: 4–6 servings

4 homemade *tofu* burgers (see page 52)
1 cake of grilled *tofu* (*yaki-dofu*)
1 cake of deep-fried *tofu* cutlet (*atsuage*)
2 deep-fried *tofu* pouches (*aburaage*)
4 eggs
¹/₂ oz (14 g) gourd strips (*kanpyo*), softened (see page 53)
Pinch of salt
3¹/₄ in (8.5 cm) long *daikon* radish
1 carrot

1 cake of *konnyaku* (devil's tongue)
4 in (10 cm) square kelp (*kombu*)
Other optional ingredients
Fish balls, fish cakes, root vegetables
Cooking broth
⎧ 5 C *dashi* stock
⎪ 2 T sugar
⎪ 3 T *sake*
⎨ 1¹/₂ T soy sauce
⎪ 2 t light soy sauce
⎪ 1 T *mirin*
⎩ 1 t salt

1. Cut grilled *tofu* into triangles. Cook deep-fried *tofu* cutlet and *tofu* pouches in ample amount of boiling ↗ water for a minute. Drain on paper towels. And cut into triangles. Cut *konnyaku* into triangles; cook in boiling water for a minute.
2. Flatten out *tofu* pouches with rolling pin for easy opening. Cut into halves, and open *tofu* pouches with thumb. Break egg into a bag of *tofu* pouch; tie opening with softened gourd strip.
3. Cut *daikon* radish into ³/₄ in (2 cm) thick round; ↗ peel skin and trim. Peel carrot and slice diagonally or flower cut.
4. Cook *daikon* and carrot in separate sauce pan until soft.
5. Wipe off white powder from kelp (see page 25); cut into half.
6. In Dutch oven, heat cooking broth and add *daikon*, carrot, *konnyaku* and kelp and cook over high heat until boiling. ↗

7. Add grilled *tofu, tofu* cutlet, egg stuffed *tofu* pouches; simmer for 20 to 30 minutes over low heat.

Other suggested ingredients

CHILLED *TOFU* —JAPANESE STYLE— (*Hiyayakko*)

This low-calorie, high protein dish can be served anytime.

INGREDIENTS: 1 serving

10¹/₂–12 oz (300–340 g) firm or soft *tofu*, well drained and chilled
Condiments
Soy sauce, Hot bean paste, Sesame oil

Place *tofu* in an individual bowl and place garnishes onto *tofu*. Serve with condiments.

Suggested Garnishes

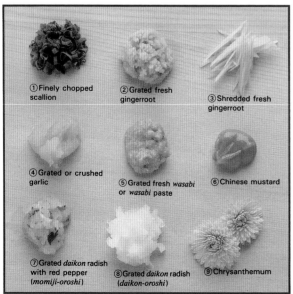

① Finely chopped scallion

② Grated fresh gingerroot

③ Shredded fresh gingerroot

④ Grated or crushed garlic

⑤ Grated fresh *wasabi* or *wasabi* paste

⑥ Chinese mustard

⑦ Grated *daikon* radish with red pepper (*momiji-oroshi*)

⑧ Grated *daikon* radish (*daikon-oroshi*)

⑨ Chrysanthemum

⑩ Stems of flowering seed pods (*hana hojiso*)

⑪ Tiny sprouts (*mejiso*)

⑫ *Benitade*

⑬ *Shiso* leaves

⑭ *Nori* seaweed

⑮ Dried bonito flakes

⑯ Toasted sesame seeds

⑰ 7-spice powder (*shichimi-togarashi*)

⑱ *Kinome*

CHILLED *TOFU* —CHINESE STYLE— (*Hiyayakko*)

The assortment of garnishes is eye appealing and will whet your appetite.

1. Place chopped scallion and shrimp onto *tofu*.
2. Mix hot bean paste with sesame oil; pour over *tofu*.
3. Pour soy sauce around *tofu*.

1 cube 10$^1/_2$–12 oz (300–340 g)
   well chilled firm *tofu*
1 t   chopped scallion
$^1/_2$ t dried shrimp, softened,
   chopped
$^1/_4$ t hot bean paste
$^1/_8$ t sesame oil
1 T   soy sauce

TOFU TERIYAKI STEAK

This marinade sauce can also be used with meat or fish. Beef _teriyaki_ is the most popular version in America.

28 oz (800 g), 14 oz (400 g) each firm _tofu_, well drained
Teriyaki sauce
- 3 T _sake_
- 2 T light soy sauce
- 1 t sesame oil
- 1 clove garlic, crushed
- 1 stalk green onion, chopped
4 T vegetable oil
7-spice powder (optional)
Chopped green onion (optional)

1. Cut _tofu_ crosswise into thirds; then cut into halves.
2. Marinate _tofu_ in _teriyaki_ sauce for 20–30 minutes.

3. Heat 2 T oil in 12 in (30 cm) skillet over medium heat; add _tofu_ pieces and stir fry until golden brown on both sides. Repeat until all _tofu_ is stir fried.
4. Sprinkle 7-spice powder and chopped green onion if you desire.

SPICY GRILLED *TOFU*

Toasted sesame seeds and sesame seed oil give a fragrant flavors while hot chili peppers bring a fiery flavors to this dish.

INGREDIENTS: 4 servings

21 oz (600 g) firm *tofu*, well drained
Hot marinade sauce
- 3 T soy sauce
- 1/3 oz (10 g) hot green pepper, chopped
- 1 T minced green onion
- 1 t crushed garlic
- 1 t ground chili pepper
- 1 t roasted sesame seeds
- 1 t sesame oil

Flour for dusting
Salt & pepper
2 T vegetable oil

1. Cut *tofu* crosswise into halves, then cut into quarters.

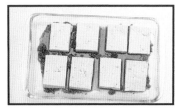

2. Mix all marinade sauce ingredients together.
3. Marinate *tofu* pieces for 30 minutes, turning once.

4. Drain off excess marinade sauce from *tofu*; coat with flour.
5. Heat 1 T oil in 12 in (30 cm) skillet over medium high heat; grill *tofu* until golden brown on both sides. Add oil if necessary.
6. Place onto serving platter.
7. Heat leftover marinade sauce in skillet and pour over *tofu*.

21

BROILED *TOFU* (*Tofu-dengaku*)

This is one of Japan's popular ways of broiling *tofu*. An irresistible topping of *miso* is characteristic of this dish.

INGREDIENTS: 4 servings

14–21 oz (300–600 g) firm *tofu*, well drained

Basting sauce A
- 4 T red *miso*
- 2 T *mirin*
- 3 T sugar
- 1 T *sake*
- Some sesame seeds

Basting sauce B
- 4 T white *miso*
- 2 T *mirin*
- 2 T sugar
- Some minced parsley

Basting sauce C
- 4¹/₂ T red *miso*
- 2 T white *miso*
- 2 T sugar
- 1 T *dashi* stock
- 1 t lime juice

1. Preheat oven to 400°F (205°C).
2. Prepare each basting sauce. Set aside.

3. Cut *tofu* into ³/₄ in (2 cm) thick slices.
4. Place on lightly greased cookie sheet; bake in oven for 5 minutes or until lightly browned.
5. Brush over tops with respective basting sauces; return to oven; bake for 3 to 4 minutes.
6. Serve with bamboo sticks.

NOTE: Soak bamboo sticks in water if you barbecue or grill over charcoal.

TOFU TEMPURA *(Agedashi-dofu)*

It must be served piping hot. Provide garnishes of your choice for dipping sauce.

INGREDIENTS: 4 servings

21 oz (600 g) firm *tofu*, well drained
³/₄–1 C all-purpose flour

3 C oil for deep-frying (350°F/ 175°C)

Tempura sauce
- 1½ C *dashi* stock
- 4 T soy sauce
- 1 T *mirin*

Garnishes
- 4 T grated *daikon* radish
- 4 t grated fresh gingerroot
- 2 t chopped green onion
- 7-spice powder
- ½ oz (15 g) dried bonito flakes

1. Cut *tofu* into 1 in (2.5 cm) thick slices.

2. Heat deep-frying oil to 350°F (175°C). Coat *tofu* with all-purpose flour.

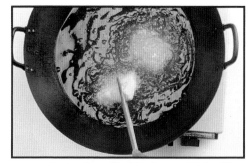

3. Deep-fly in oil until golden brown. Drain. Place in individual dishes.
4. Heat *tempura* sauce to a boil; pour over *tofu*.
5. Sprinkle garnishes of your choice or serve with *tofu*.

23

TOFU HOT POT (*Yu-dofu*)

One of the easiest of all Japanese *tofu* dishes. It can be prepared in minutes and is often served as a main dish in Japan.

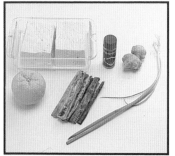

INGREDIENTS: 4 servings

24 oz (685 g) firm or soft *tofu*
2 4 in (10 cm) square kelp (*kombu*)
Garnishes
2 T fresh grated gingerroot
2 green onions, finely chopped
7-spice powder
Yuzu citron, lime or lemon wedges
Dipping sauces
Lemon dressing, Sesame dressing, Hoisin sauce dressing, Soy sauce dressing

Dipping sauces

Lemon dressing

¹/₂ C lemon juice
¹/₂ C soy sauce

Sesame dressing

²/₃ C toasted and
ground white sesame
seeds
2¹/₂ T soy sauce
3 T sugar
2 T *dashi* stock

Hoisin sauce dressing

¹/₃ C Hoisin sauce
¹/₂ t sesame oil
1 T *dashi* stock

Soy sauce dressing

4 T soy sauce
1 T *sake* or *mirin*
3 T *dashi* stock
¹/₄ C dried bonito
flakes

Mix all soy sauce ingredients and bring to a boil. Set aside.

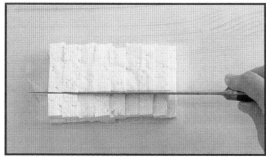

1. Cut *tofu* into 1 in (2.5 cm) cubes.

2. Wipe off white powder from kelp; make 3–4 slashes with knife.

3. Prepare each dipping sauce (see above).
4. In large Dutch oven or earthen casserole dish, place kelp and fill ²/₃ full with water.
5. Bring to a boil; add *tofu* pieces.
6. Serve with dipping sauces or place soy sauce dressing in a casserole dish and dip *tofu*.

SEASONED FROZEN *TOFU* (*Koya-dofu no fukumeni*)

INGREDIENTS: 4 servings

Slow simmering makes this dish nutritious.

2 cubes HOMEMADE FROZEN *TOFU*
  (see page 27) or commercially
  made frozen *tofu* (*Koya-dofu*)
3¹/₂ oz (100 g) pea pods, cooked
Some *yuzu* citron or lime peel

Cooking broth

⎧ 1³/₄ C *dashi* stock
⎪ 3¹/₂ T sugar
⎨ 1 T *sake*
⎪ 1 t salt
⎩ 1 T *mirin*

1 t light soy sauce

1. If you use commercially made *tofu*, soak in boiling water for 20 minutes with drop lid; change water until most of water turn to clear.
2. Cut frozen *tofu* into fourths.
3. In Dutch oven or 3-quart saucepan, heat cooking broth to a boil; add frozen *tofu*. Bring to a boil. Reduce heat to

medium-low and cook another 20 minutes.
4. Add light soysauce. Turn off heat and leave on stove for one hour.
5. Place *tofu* in bowls and put cooked pea pods on top. Pour over some cooking broth.
6. Sprinkle some lime or *yuzu* citron peel.

NOTE: Green beans can be substituted for pea pods.

The secret flavoring agents in this recipe are *dashi* stock* and *mirin* *; combined with sugar, *sake*, salt and a touch of light soy sauce*.

*Seasonings can be found at Oriental grocery stores and large supermarkets.

HOMEMADE FROZEN *TOFU* (*Koya-dofu*)

INGREDIENTS:
Makes 2 14 oz (400g) cubes each

2 14 oz (400g) each firm *tofu*

1. Drain *tofu* well. Place *tofu* on several layer of towels on cutting board, and top with water-filled bowl or some weight. Change towels often.

2. Wrap with plastic wrap.
3. Place on bamboo mat. Keep in freezer for several hours or overnight. ✓

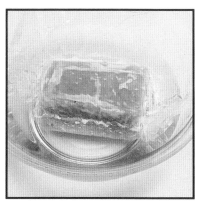

4. Frozen *tofu* is umber color. Dip in water; remove plastic wrap.

5. For cooking, rinse in water first, then follow instructions.

TOFU FISH SAUCE

It adds a festive touch to many fish dishes.

8 oz (225 g) soft *tofu*, well drained
2 T small Japanese cucumber, finely chopped or ¹/₂ seeded and peeled cucumber, chopped
1 t horseradish mustard
1 t grated onion
³/₄ t dried dillweed
¹/₂ t lemon juice
¹/₂ t minced garlic
1 t light soy sauce
1 t salt

1. Whip *tofu* until smooth.
2. Combine *tofu* and all ingredients.
3. Chill, covered, until ready to serve.

NOTE: Quick *Tofu* **Fish Sauce** is good for Norway sardine, salmon, Atlantic mackerel, albacore tuna, sablefish, herring, rainbow trout, other white meat fish and oysters.

STEAMED FISH WITH *TOFU*

Tofu **fish sauce gives this dish its vibrant flavor and character.**

4 firm fish fillets, about 3 oz (85 g) each
1 t *sake*
$^1/_2$ t salt
$^1/_8$ t pepper
$10^1/_2$ oz (300 g) *tofu*
4 *shiitake* mushrooms, softened and trimmed stem ends
1 T thinly sliced fresh gingerroot
2 green onions
1 T *sake*

1. Sprinkle *sake*, salt & pepper on fish fillets; place in heatproof dishes . Cut *tofu* into $1^1/_2$ in (4 cm) cubes. ↙

2. Slice *shiitake* mushrooms into $1^1/_8$–$1^1/_2$ in (3–4 cm) thick slices. Cut green onion into $1^1/_8$–$1^1/_2$ in (3–4 cm) long pieces.

3. Place *tofu, shiitake* mushrooms, gingerroot and green onion in dishes. ↙

4. Sprinkle *sake* and steam for 10 to 12 minutes over high heat.
5. Serve with fish sauce. (See page 28)

STIR-FRIED SEAFOOD AND VEGETABLES

The artfully composed ingredients, assortment of seafoods and vegetables, are stir fried with special sauce.

INGREDIENTS: 4 servings

21 oz (600 g) firm *tofu*, well drained
2–3 T vegetable oil
3¹/₂ oz (100 g) squid
1 t *sake*
¹/₈ t salt
2 t cornstarch

3¹/₂ oz (100 g) raw shrimp, shelled, deveined
A { ¹/₂ t ginger juice, juice from grated fresh gingerroot
1 t *sake*
¹/₈ t salt

1 green onion, cut into 1¹/₈–1¹/₂ in (3–4 cm) long pieces
1 T chopped gingerroot
2¹/₂ oz (70 g) bamboo shoots, shredded
2¹/₂ oz (70 g) carrot, shredded
1¹/₂ C small broccoli flowerets, cooked or 2¹/₂ oz (70 g) Chinese cabbage, shredded
6 dried *shiitake* mushrooms, softened and cut into halves
8 hard boiled quail eggs or 2 hard boiled eggs, cut into wedges

B { ²/₃ C chicken stock
1 T *sake*
1 t sugar
¹/₂ T soy sauce
¹/₂ t salt
20 pea pods
1 T cornstarch plus 2 T water for thickening
¹/₈ t sesame oil

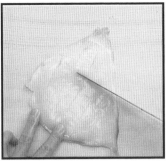

1. Remove the outer skin from squid.

2. Make slanting incisions so that squid will not shrink after cooking.

3. Sprinkle *sake* and salt; coat with cornstarch. Dip into boiling water for 30 seconds. Drain and set aside.

4. Cut into 1 in (2.5 cm) square cubes.

5. Marinate shrimp in ingredients **A**.

6. Cut *tofu* crosswise into halves; then cut into 1/2–3/4 in (1.5–2 cm) thick slices.

7. Prepared vegetables.

8. Sauté *tofu* in 1–2 T oil on both sides until light brown. Set aside.

9. Heat 1 T oil in wok over high heat; add shrimp and stir fry for a minute. Set aside.

12. Add squid, shrimp, *tofu* and boiled quail eggs.

10. Add 1 T oil if necessary to wok; stir fry green onion and gingerroot for 30 seconds.

11. Add bamboo shoots, carrot, broccoli or Chinese cabbage and *shiitake* mushrooms; stir fry until vegetables are soft, about 5 minutes over medium-high heat.

13. Add ingredients **B**; bring to a boil. Add pea pods and cook for a minute or until pea pods turn into bright color. Pour in cornstarch mixture and stir well; add 1/8 t sesame oil. Remove from heat.

NOTE: Garnish with hard boiled eggs if you can't obtain quail eggs recipe calls for.

STIR-FRIED OYSTERS AND *TOFU*

This low-calorie, high-protein dish can be ideal for calorie cautious people.

INGREDIENTS: 4 servings

21 oz (600 g) firm *tofu*, well drained
14 oz (400 g) fresh oysters
16 pea pods or $^1/_3$ C green peas
3 dried *shiitake* mushrooms or $^3/_4$ C sliced fresh mushrooms
$^1/_2$ bunch green onion, cut into 1 in (2.5 cm) long pieces
2 t minced fresh gingerroot
2 T vegetable oil
Sauce
$^1/_2$ t hot bean paste
$1^1/_2$ T red *miso*
2 t *mirin* or sugar
$1^1/_2$ T *sake* or sweet sherry
$^1/_2$ t cornstarch plus 1 t *shiitake* soaking liquid or water

1. Cut *tofu* crosswise into halves, then slice into $^1/_2$ in (1.5 cm) thick pieces.

2. Clean oysters in salted water; drain. Dip into boiling water for 30 seconds; drain well.

3. Trim off hard ends from pea pods. Soften *shiitake* mushrooms and cut off stem ends; cut into $^1/_2$ in (1.5 cm) cubes.
4. Mix all sauce ingredients. Set aside.

5. Heat 1 T oil in wok over high heat; add pea pods and stir fry for 30 seconds. Remove from wok and set aside.

6. Add 1 T oil to wok and add gingerroot; stir fry for 30 seconds over medium-high heat. Add *shiitake* mushrooms or fresh mushrooms and oysters and stir fry for 30 seconds.

7. Put in *tofu* and toss lightly; add sauce and green onion; bring to a boil.
8. Thicken with cornstarch mixture. Add pea pods; stir to serve.

SAUTÉED SHRIMP WITH HOISIN SAUCE

INGREDIENTS: 4 servings

A
- 3 T Hoisin sauce*
- 2 T rice vinegar
- 2 T water
- 2 t sugar
- $1/2$ t ground ginger
- $1/2$ t cornstarch
- $1/8$ t crushed red pepper

2 T vegetable oil

14 oz (400 g) firm *tofu*, well drained, cut into 1 in (2.5 cm) cubes

$1/2$ lb (225 g) medium size (15–17 count) raw shrimp, shelled & deveined

1 clove garlic, minced or pressed

6 green onions, cut diagonally in 1 in (2.5 cm) lengths

Hoisin sauce – one of the most important ingredients in many Chinese dishes – brings to this dish something special.

*Available at most large supermarkets or Oriental grocery stores.

1. Combine ingredients **A**; set aside.

2. Heat 1 T oil in a large skillet over medium-high heat; add *tofu* cubes and stir fry about 2 minutes or till lightly browned all sides. Remove from the skillet and set aside.

3. Add 1 T oil to a skillet. Stir fry garlic, shrimp for 2 minutes over medium-high heat, stirring constantly.

4. Stir in the green onion and Hoisin sauce mixture **A** and cook, stirring until thickened and shrimp are opaque throughout, about 3 minutes.

5. Add *tofu* and combine well.

33

CRABMEAT AND *TOFU* PATTIES

This quick and easy recipe is a fine one to keep in mind for unexpected guests.

INGREDIENTS: 4 servings

21 oz (600g) firm *tofu,* well drained
1 egg, beaten
1 t lemon juice
4 T *panko* (dehydrated bread crumbs)
$1/2$ t salt
Dash of pepper
1 can (6 oz/170g) crabmeat, drained and cartilage removed
2 oz (60g) fresh mushrooms or canned mushrooms
2 T vegetable oil

1. Crumble well drained *tofu.* Mix with egg, lemon juice, bread crumbs, salt and pepper.

2. Chop fresh mushrooms. Combine *tofu,* crabmeat and mushrooms. Divide into eighths.

3. Make patties, $3/4$ in (1 cm) thick. Heat 2 T oil in 12 in (30cm) skillet over medium-high heat and grill patties on both sides until golden brown, 5 minutes each.

TUNA ROLLS

2 14 oz (400 g) each firm *tofu*, well drained
1 6$^1/_2$ oz (185 g) tuna can, drained
1 T mayonnaise
1 t chopped onion
4 T spinach leaves, chopped
4 large sheet *nori* seaweed
Some cornstarch for dusting
Sauce
$^2/_3$ C *dashi* or chicken stock
$^1/_2$ t salt
1 T light soy sauce
1 t *sake*
$^1/_2$ T cornstarch plus 1 T water
Lemon peel as garnish

Nearly everyone's favorite tuna is mildly seasoned with soy sauce dressing.

1. Cut *tofu* into fourths as shown.

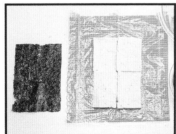

2. Place plastic wrap on a bamboo mat and place *tofu*. Sprinkle cornstarch on surface of *tofu*.

3. Cut *nori* seaweed into same size as *tofu*. Place on *tofu*. Mix tuna with mayonnaise and divide into half. Place tuna onto *nori* as shown.

4. Place chopped spinach.
5. Roll up and tie both ends with rubber bands. Repeat for other roll.

6. Place rolls in hot steaming steamer; steam for 10 minutes over medium heat. ↗

7. Heat sauce ingredients in a saucepan until sauce thickens.
8. Cut rolls into fourths with wrap on.
9. Remove plastic wrap. Place into an individual bowl. Pour sauce over and garnish with some lemon peel.

STEAMED *TOFU* WITH SHRIMP

Steamed *tofu* is an ideal dish to prepare for a buffet party.

INGREDIENTS: Makes 1 loaf

6 × 5¹/₂ × 1³/₄ in (15 × 13.5 × 4.7 cm)

21 oz (600 g) firm *tofu*, well drained

1 egg white, beaten
1 t all-purpose flour

A {
Some vegetable oil and all-purpose flour for coating
4¹/₄ oz (120 g) raw shrimp, shelled, deveined
4 T green peas, cooked or frozen
1 can (4 oz/115 g) sliced mushrooms, drained and chopped
1 egg yolk
1 t *sake*
¹/₂ t salt
}

Sauce
{
1¹/₄ C *dashi* or chicken stock
1 t *mirin*
1 T *sake*
1¹/₂ T light soy sauce
¹/₂ T cornstarch plus 1 T water for thickening
}

Condiments
Chinese mustard
Soy sauce
Hot chili sesame oil

1. Crumble *tofu*; mix with egg white and flour.

2. Chop shrimp; mix with other ingredients **A**.

3. Coat thin film of oil in a mold; dust with flour.

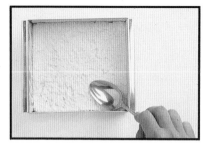

4. Put in half portion of *tofu* mixture.

5. Add shrimp mixture on top. Smooth out surface.

6. Place other half portion of *tofu* mixture; flatten out.

7. Steam for 20 minutes over high heat. Add water if necessary during steaming. Let it sit for 5 minutes before slicing.
8. Heat sauce in a small saucepan over high heat until it boils; add cornstarch mixture.
9. Slice *tofu* and serve on platter and pour sauce over.

Oven baking method

Preheat oven to 400°F (205°C). Fill ²/₃ water in baking pan and place mold. Bake in oven for 18 minutes or until *tofu* and shrimp are cooked.

TOFU WITH SHRIMP

This masterpiece *tofu* dish can be prepared quickly on festive occasions. Garnish it artfully with coriander (Chinese parsley).

INGREDIENTS: 4 servings

2 14 oz (400 g) each firm *tofu*, well drained
Cornstarch for coating
1/3 lb (150 g) raw shrimp, shelled, deveined
1/4 t salt
4 t *sake*
1 t cornstarch
1 green onion, chopped
1 t fresh gingerroot, chopped

A {
  1 cube chicken bouillon
  2/3 C water
  2 T each soy sauce, *sake*
  1 t sugar
}

2 T vegetable oil
1 T cornstarch plus 2 T water for thickening
Coriander as garnish

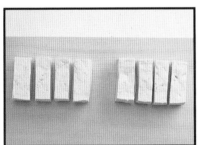

1. Cut each *tofu* into four or six rectangular pieces.

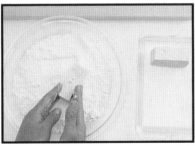

2. Dust each pieces with cornstarch lightly.

3. Clean shrimp and chop finely; mix 1/2 t salt, 4 t *sake* and 1 t cornstarch.

4. Place shrimp between *tofu* pieces as shown.

5. In 12 in (30 cm) skillet, heat 2 T oil over medium-high heat; add chopped green onion and gingerroot. Sauté for a minute. Add ingredients **A** and bring to a boil.

6. Add *tofu* and shrimp carefully with spatula; cover and simmer until shrimp is cooked, about 15 minutes.

7. Add cornstarch mixture for thickening.

8. Sprinkle chopped coriander on top.

STEAMED BEAN CURD ROLLS (*Yubamakimushi*)

This dish should be served at an intimate party.

INGREDIENTS: 4 servings

4 sheets (8 in/20 cm square each) dried bean curd (*yuba*)
1 can (6 oz/170 g) crabmeat, drained and cartilage removed
6 oz (170 g) cocktail shrimp, chopped
4 oz (115 g) ground chicken or lean pork

A
- 1 small egg, beaten
- 2 T chopped green onion
- 2 T soy sauce
- 1 T *sake*
- 2 T cornstarch
- 1/2 t sesame oil
- 1 t sugar

1 T cornstarch plus 1/2 T water for thickening

1. Soak dried beancurd sheets in lukewarm water until soft, about 2 minutes.

2. Grind ground meat until smooth or chop with knife.

3. In a large bowl mix ingredients **A** with chopped shrimp, ground meat and crabmeat.

4. Divide into fourths.

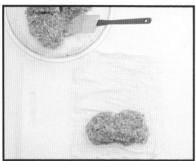  

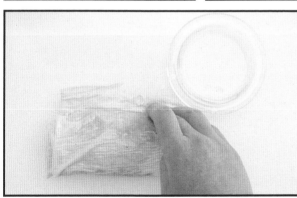

5. Pat dry bean curd sheets. Place the filling onto the sheet as shown; roll carefully. Wet the edge of the sheet with cornstarch mixture and enclose the ends. Repeat other sheets.

6. Lightly oil steamer rack and place rolls seamside down. Steam for 20 minutes over high heat.

7. Cut into serving size.

VARIATION   FRIED BEAN CURD ROLLS

The recipe suggests the memorable flavor of the bean curd and fillings.

Heat oil to 350°F (175°C). Fry **STEAMED BEAN CURD ROLLS** until golden brown. Drain on wire rack. Cut and serve.

STUFFED ROLLED CHICKEN

This tasty chicken dish, resembles the chicken Cordon Bleu, is zesty and soothing. The chicken rolls are crisp on the outside, soft and tender inside.

Microwave cooking
1½ quart glass baking dish or 9 in (23 cm) glass pie dish
2 whole chicken breast, skinned and boned
2 T *sake* or cooking wine
10–12 oz (285–340 g) *tofu*, well drained
⅛ t each salt & pepper
1 T minced parsley
6 oz (170 g) shredded mozzarella cheese
All-purpose flour for coating
1 can (10¾ oz) condensed cream of mushroom soup
2 T oil

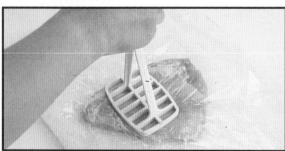

1. Cut each breast in halves.
2. Place between 2 pieces plastic wrap; pound with mallet or side of saucer until ¼ in (7 mm) thick, not tear meat. Or butter fly each half by slicing breast from the outer edge, part way through, to open like a book. Sprinkle *sake* or cooking wine.

3. Crumble *tofu* with fork.

4. Add salt, pepper and parsley. Divide into fourths.

5. Place *tofu* onto chicken breast.

6. Roll up and secure with a tooth pick.

7. Coat rolled chicken with flour.
8. Heat oil in 12 in (30 cm) skillet over medium high heat; add chicken.
9. Cook until all sides get lightly browned.

10. Place chicken pieces into baking dish; pour condensed cream of mushroom soup and ¹/₄ can of water.
11. Sprinkle shredded mozzarella cheese on top and cover with plastic wrap.

12. Cook on full power for 10 minutes.
13. Turn pieces over; continue to cook 5 minutes or until they fork tender.
14. Allow to stand 5 minutes before serving. Remove tooth picks.

CHICKEN AND *TOFU* WITH HOT BEAN SAUCE

21 oz (600g) firm *tofu*, well drained
14 oz (400g) chicken thigh
$^1/_2$ t each soy sauce, *sake*

$^1/_2$ oz (14g) gingerroot, sliced thin
1 clove garlic, chopped
1 can (8$^1/_2$ oz/240g) sliced bamboo shoots, drained
4 *shiitake* mushrooms
1 lb (450g) bok choy (Chinese cabbage) or other Chinese greens, cut into 2 in (5cm) long pieces
1 green onion, cut into 2 in (5cm) long pieces
1$^1/_2$ t hot bean paste
1 C chicken broth or 1 cup water with 1 cube chicken bouillon
A $\begin{cases} 2 \text{ T soy sauce} \\ 2 \text{ T } sake \\ 1 \text{ t sugar} \\ \text{A dash of pepper} \end{cases}$
2 T vegetable oil
1 T cornstarch plus 2 T water for thickening

Fresh gingerroot, garlic and hot bean sauce bring the fiery flavors to this chicken dish. A side serving of hot cooked rice provides a welcome accompaniment.

1. Cut *tofu* into 1 in (2.5cm) cubes.
2. Cut chicken into serving pieces; mix with soy sauce and *sake*. Set aside.
3. Soak *shiitake* mushrooms until soft; trim hard stem ends. Slice thin.
4. Heat 1 T oil in wok over high heat; stir fry *tofu* until lightly browned all sides, 2 to 3 minutes. Set aside.
5. Add 1 T oil to wok; add hot bean paste, gingerroot and garlic. Stir fry for a few minutes; add chicken and stir fry until color changes to white.

6. Add bamboo shoots, *shiitake* mushrooms, bok choy and green onion; stir fry for 3 to 4 minutes.

7. Pour chicken broth and bring to a boil; add ingredients **A**.

8. Mix well and add *tofu* and cornstarch mixture for thickening.

NOTE: Cashew or peanuts can be added to this dish.

CHICKEN WITH STEAMED *TOFU*

21 oz (600 g) *tofu*
3¹/₂ oz (100 g) chicken, skinned and boned

A { 1 egg white, lightly beaten
¹/₂ t salt
1 t *sake*
1 t sesame oil
1 T cornstarch

1 bunch green onion, sliced
4 small *shiitake* mushrooms, softened and sliced
8–12 pea pods
1 T chopped fresh gingerroot
4 C oil for deep-frying (350°F/ 175°C)

B { 1¹/₄ C chicken stock
¹/₄ t salt
¹/₂ t sugar
1 T *sake*

1 t cornstarch plus 2 t water for thickening
¹/₂ t sesame oil

This colorful dish is the ideal for casual entertaining. The combination of *tofu*, chicken and Chinese pea pods provides a textural contrast. Serve with steamed rice or noodles.

1. Steam *tofu* for 20 minutes over high heat in a steamer. Cut *tofu* into ¹/₄ in × 1¹/₄ in (0.7 cm × 3 cm) pieces.

2. Cut chicken into serving pieces. Mix ingredients **A**; toss with chicken pieces.

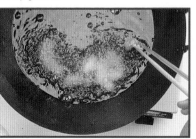

3. Heat deep frying oil in wok to 350°F (175°C), deep fry chicken pieces until light brown. Set aside.

4. Remove oil except 1 T from wok; add gingerroot, green onion, *shiitake* mushrooms and pea pods and stir fry over high heat for a minute.

5. Add ingredients **B**, chicken and *tofu* and bring to a boil. Pour in cornstarch mixture and stir well. Turn off heat and add sesame oil.

43

BRAISED CHICKEN AND CHESTNUTS

The chicken is enhanced by the flavor of chestnuts.

INGREDIENTS: 4 servings

$10^1/_2$–14 oz (300–400 g) firm *tofu*, well drained

$1^1/_2$–2 lbs (685–900 g) broiler-fryer chicken, cut up

1 T *sake*

1 T soy sauce

1 T gingerroot, shredded

8 oz (225 g) chestnuts (canned chestnuts in syrup)

4 T vegetable oil

A {
4 T soy sauce
2 T *sake*
$1^1/_2$ t sugar
$^3/_4$ C water
}

1. Cut *tofu* into $^3/_4$ in × $1^1/_2$ in (2 cm × 4 cm) pieces.
2. Marinate chicken in *sake* and soy sauce mixture for 15 minutes.

3. Heat 2 T oil in wok over medium high heat and add *tofu*; stir fry until brown on both sides. Set aside.

4. Add 2 T oil to wok and stir fry gingerroot and chicken over high heat until chicken turns to whitish color.

5. Add chestnuts with syrup and mix well.

6. In Dutch oven, add ingredients **A** and chicken and chestnuts and bring to a boil. Cover and reduce heat to low and cook for 40 minutes.

7. Add *tofu* and cook another 5 minutes. Remove from heat.

BRAISED BEEF AND *TOFU*

INGREDIENTS: 4 servings

¹/₂ lb (225g) *sukiyaki* meat or
   thin sliced beef
21 oz (600g) firm *tofu*, cut into
   1 in (2.5cm) cubes
1 can yam noodles (*shirataki*),
   drained
2 green onions, cut into 1¹/₂ in
   (4cm) diagonal pieces
1 T chopped gingerroot

A
   ¹/₂ C water
   ¹/₄ C soy sauce
   2¹/₂ T sugar
   2 T *mirin*

2 T vegetable oil

This quick and savory method of cooking *tofu* is everyone's favorite. It is similar to *sukiyaki*, one of the popular Japanese dishes.

1. Cut *sukiyaki* meat into 1–1¹/₂ in (2.5–4cm) long pieces.
2. Heat wok; add 2 T oil and stir fry gingerroot for 30 seconds over high heat.
3. Add meat; stir fry until color changes.
4. Add drained yam noodles and ingredients **A**; bring to a boil.

5. Add *tofu*; cook for 5 minutes over medium heat.
6. Add green onion; cook 1 to 2 minutes. Turn off heat.

NOTE: For one meal dish, pour beaten egg over cooked meat. Serve on hot cooked rice.

STIR-FRIED *TOFU* WITH GROUND BEEF

Try this dish when time is limited. Soy sauce and *miso*, traditional Japanese seasonings for many centuries, enhance the flavor of this dish.

INGREDIENTS: 4 servings

14 oz (400 g) firm *tofu*, well drained and cut into 1 in (2.5 cm) cubes
1 bunch green onion, cut into 1 1/2 in (4 cm) lengths
1 T minced fresh gingerroot
1 clove garlic, minced
1 medium onion, cut into half, then sliced thin
{ 1/2 lb (225 g) ground beef
{ 1 T all-purpose flour

3 T oil
A { 1/2 C chicken stock
{ 1 t *miso*
{ 2 T soy sauce
{ 1 t sugar
1 t cornstarch plus 2 t water for thickening

1. Mix all ingredients **A** together; set aside. Mix ground beef and all-purpose flour. Heat wok; add 1 T oil. Stir fry green onion until soft over high heat. Remove from wok and set aside.

2. Add 2 T oil to wok and stir fry gingerroot and garlic for 30 seconds over high heat; add onion slices and ground meat. Stir fry until color changes to white.

3. Add *tofu* and pour in **A**; bring to a boil. Add cooked green onion. Add cornstarch mixture to thicken.

CURRY FLAVORED CHINESE-STYLE *TOFU*

A touch of curry powder brings a refreshing flavor to the familiar combination of *tofu* and ground meat.

INGREDIENTS: 4 servings

14 oz (400 g) firm *tofu*
4 dried *shiitake* mushrooms, softened
  and with stem ends trimmed off
1/2 lb (225 g) ground lean pork or
  beef
A { 1 t soy sauce
    { 1/2 t sugar
    { 1 t *sake*
2 green onions, chopped
1 T chopped fresh gingerroot
2 dried hot pepper, seeds removed
  and chopped
2 T oil for stir frying
1 T sesame oil
1/2 t curry powder
1 cube bouillon, chicken or beef
1 C hot water
1/2 C cooked peas
1 t cornstarch plus 2 t water for
  thickening

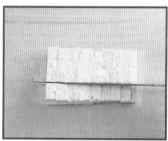

1. Boil *tofu* in boiling water for 30 seconds; drain on papertowels. Cut into 3/4 in (2 cm) cubes.

2. Slice softened *shiitake* mushrooms. Mix ground meat with ingredients **A**.

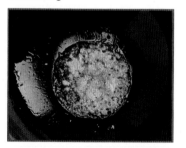

3. Heat wok and add 2 T oil; stir fry green onion, gingerroot and hot pepper for a few seconds over high heat.

4. Add ground meat; stir fry until gray. Add curry powder and sesame oil and stir fry until well mixed. Dissolve 1 bouillon cube in hot water; pour into meat mixture; bring to a boil over medium heat.

5. Add *tofu* and *shiitake* mushrooms. Add peas and thicken with cornstarch mixture over medium heat.

NOTE: Increase portion of curry powder if you desire. Soft *tofu* can be used instead of firm *tofu*. Cut into a little larger sizes.

PORK AND *TOFU* SZECHUAN STYLE

INGREDIENTS: 4 servings

21 oz (600g) firm *tofu*, well drained

2 *shiitake* mushrooms, softened and sliced

1 C sliced bamboo shoots

6 oz (170g) pea pods or 1 package (6 oz/170g) frozen pea pods, cooked

1 green onion, cut diagonally into ³/₄ in (2cm) pieces

3 dried hot pepper, coarsely chopped

1 clove garlic, coarsely chopped

1 T coarsely chopped fresh gingerroot

3 T oil for stir frying

A { 8 oz (225g) pork boneless loin or boneless shoulder
1 t *sake*
1 t soy sauce

B { 1 T each *miso*, *sake*
4 T soy sauce
1 t sugar

Szechuan is one of the five main cooking regions of China. This recipe perhaps most typifies the cooking of Szechuan.

1. Cut *tofu* into about ¹/₂ in (1.5cm) thick slices. Mix ingredients **A** together; set aside. Mix ingredients **B**; set aside.

2. Heat 1–2 T oil in 12 in (30cm) skillet over medium-high heat, add *tofu* and stir fry *tofu* pieces until lightly browned. Set aside.

3. Add 1 T oil to the skillet. Stir fry hot pepper, garlic, green onion and gingerroot for 1 minute. Add pork; stir fry for 2 to 3 minutes over medium-high heat.

4. Add *shiitake* mushrooms, bamboo shoots and pea pods; stir fry 2 minutes.

5. Add *tofu*; toss together carefully.

6. Pour ingredients **B** and mix carefully not to break *tofu*. Turn off heat.

PORK AND *TOFU* WITH HOT CHILI SAUCE

Serve this dish with hot cooked rice or bean thread (cellophane) noodles.

1 cube (12 oz/340 g) deep-fried
tofu cutlet (*atsuage*)
1 lb (450 g) pork tenderloin or
boneless loin

A {
1²/₃ C water
6¹/₂ T *sake*
¹/₄ leek, cut into 2–3 pieces
¹/₂ in (1.5 cm) cube fresh
gingerroot

B {
1¹/₂ T soy sauce
2 T sesame paste (optional)
or Hoisin sauce
2 t brown sugar
1 T *sake*
¹/₂–1 t hot bean paste
²/₃ C chicken stock

2 T cornstarch plus 4 T water
1 T toasted white sesame seeds

1. Dip deep-fried *tofu* cutlet into boiling water for 1 minute to remove excess grease. Cut into fourths, then cut into triangle shapes.
2. Cut pork loin into 1¹/₈ in (3 cm) pieces.

3. In a 3-quart saucepan, put ingredients **A** and pork pieces; cook for 20 minutes over medium heat. Remove from heat and pick up pork pieces; set aside.

4. Discard ingredients **A** and clean the saucepan. Put pork in the pan and add ingredients **B**; cook for 20 minutes over medium heat.

5. Add *tofu* cutlet and stir; bring to a boil. Thicken with cornstarch mixture. Place in a platter and sprinkle sesame seeds on top.

50

STUFFED DEEP-FRIED *TOFU* CUTLETS

INGREDIENTS: 4 servings

4 deep-fried *tofu* cutlets (*atsuage*),
   12 oz (340 g) each
4 oz (115 g) ground lean beef
2 *shiitake* mushrooms, softened or
   2 white mushrooms, chopped
$1/2$ T chopped green onion
$1/2$ egg, beaten

A $\begin{cases} 1/2 \text{ t sugar} \\ 1 \text{ t } sake \\ 1/2 \text{ soy sauce} \end{cases}$

A pinch of salt
2 T cornstarch
Cooking broth
$\begin{cases} 3 \text{ C } dashi \text{ stock or chicken broth} \\ 1 \text{ T sugar} \\ 3 \text{ T soy sauce} \\ 1 \text{ T } mirin \\ 1/2 \text{ t salt} \end{cases}$

Deep-fried *tofu* cutlets turn into legendary Japanese delicacy.

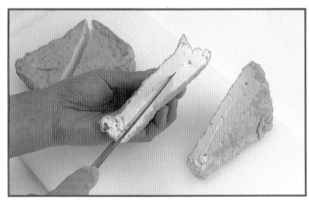

1. Dip *tofu* cutlets into boiling water for 10 seconds to remove excess grease. Drain on paper towels; cut diagonally into halves. Make slash on cut sides.
2. Mix ground beef with mushrooms, green onion and beaten egg. Mix ingredients **A**.
3. Mix meat and **A** and divide into eighths.

4. Dust cornstarch on cut sides of *tofu* cutlets; fill meat mixture in a pocket.
5. In 3-quart saucepan, heat cooking broth over medium heat; add stuffed *tofu*; cover and cook for 15 minute over medium heat.

HOMEMADE *TOFU* BURGERS (*Ganmodoki*)

INGREDIENTS: Makes 20 burgers

21–24 oz (600–685 g) firm *tofu*, well drained
3¹/₂ oz (100 g) white fish fillet
1 egg white, beaten
6 dried cloud ear mushrooms, softened and sliced
1 carrot, cooked and cut into julienne strips
2 dried *shiitake* mushrooms, softened and sliced thin
2 T toasted sesame seeds
2 T all purpose flour, sifted
Oil for deep-frying (300°F/ 150°C)

Tofu **combined with colorful vegetables and touch of toasted sesame seeds gives this dish a rich flavor.**

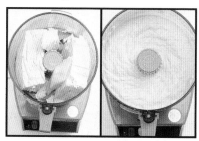

1. In a food processor, put *tofu* and fish fillet. Beat until smooth.

2. Mix with rest of ingredients.

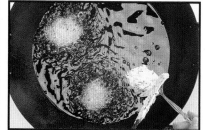

3. Heat oil to 300°F (150°C). Using 2 soup spoons, shape *tofu* into rounds (heaping tablespoon).

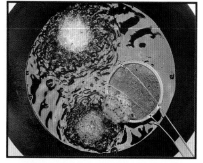

4. Deep-fry *tofu* burgers few at a time until golden or float on surface. Drain on wire rack.

SEASONED HOMEMADE *TOFU* BURGERS

Cooking broth
2¹/₂ C *dashi* stock
3 T *mirin*
¹/₄ C light soy sauce

1. Pour boiling water over deep-fried *tofu* burgers to remove excess grease.
2. In 2-quart saucepan, heat cooking broth and add *tofu* burgers; simmer for 30 minutes over low heat.

DEEP-FRIED *TOFU* POUCHES WITH VEGETABLES

8 deep-fried *tofu* pouches (*aburaage*)
$1/2$ oz (14g) dried gourd strips (*kanpyo*) (optional)
$3^1/_2$–4 oz (100–115g) ground chicken
1 oz (30g) carrot, cut into julienne strips
4 dried *shiitake* mushrooms
4 oz (100g) bean sprouts

Cooking broth
A
- $1/2$ C *dashi* stock
- 2 T *mirin*
- 2T soy sauce

Cooking broth
B
- $2^1/_2$ C *dashi* stock
- 2 T sugar
- 1 T *mirin*
- 4 T soy sauce
- $1/2$ t salt

This recipe adds a festive touch to many economy main dishes.

1. Press *tofu* pouches with rolling pin for easy opening.
2. In a large saucepan, boil 3 cups of water. Put in *tofu* pouches and cook for 1 to 2 minutes to remove excess grease. Drain well.
3. Cut in half and open *tofu* pouches with thumb as illustrated. Set aside.
4. Soak dried gourd strips in water until soft; wash in salted water (1 T salt). Rinse well.
5. Soak *shiitake* mushrooms in lukewarm water until soft. Trim off stems and slice thin. Rinse bean sprouts in water; drain well.

6. Mix cooking broth ingredients **A** in 3-quart pan; add chicken, carrot, mushrooms and bean sprouts. Cook for 15 minutes over medium heat. Drain and let it cool slightly.

7. Put the meat mixture in *tofu* pouches $2/3$ full (about $1^1/_2$ T).
8. Secure with tooth pick or tie around openning with gourd strips.

9. In 3-quart saucepan, mix cooking broth **B** and bring to a boil. Add *tofu* pouches and cook for 15 minutes over medium heat or until most of broth is gone.

53

STIR-FRIED NUTS AND EGGPLANTS

INGREDIENTS: 4 servings

1 14 oz (400 g) cube firm *tofu*, well drained
2 eggplants (small)
2 green peppers, chopped
1/3 C peanuts or cashew nuts
1 bunch green onion
1 dried red pepper
Marinade sauce
{ 1 t light soy sauce
{ 1 t fresh ginger juice (juice from grated fresh gingerroot)
2 T vegetable oil
1/2 C chicken stock
1/2 T *sake*
1 t salt
1/2 t sesame oil

Eggplants are widely used in many countries. This delightful recipe makes a colorful addition to a party menu.

1. Cut *tofu* crosswise into halves and marinate in soy sauce and ginger juice. Slice into 1/2 in (1.5 cm) thick.

2. Cut eggplants into chunks; soak in water. Cut green onion into 1 in (2.5 cm) pieces. Remove seeds from red pepper; cut into small pieces.

3. Heat 1 T oil in wok; stir fry *tofu* pieces on both sides until golden brown. Set aside. Stir fry eggplants; set aside.

4. Add 1 T oil in wok and stir fry red pepper, green onions, green peppers and nuts over medium high heat for 2–3 minutes.

5. Pour in chicken stock and add *tofu* and eggplants; stir gently. Season with *sake* and salt. Bring to a boil. Turn off heat and add sesame oil.

TOFU WITH OYSTER SAUCE

A delicately flavored oyster sauce provides a nourishing texture with *tofu*.

INGREDIENTS: 4 servings

21–24 oz (600–685 g) firm *tofu*, well drained

1 can (1³/₄ oz/50 g) mushrooms, sliced

1 C frozen mixed vegetables, cooked

2 stalks green onion

1 T fresh gingerroot, coarsely chopped

¹/₂ T soy sauce

2 T oyster sauce

2 T *sake*

¹/₂ C chicken stock

¹/₈ t pepper

1 T cornstarch plus 2–3 T water for thickening

2–3 T vegetable oil

1. Cook *tofu* in boiling water for 30 seconds; drain. Cut *tofu* crosswise into halves and slice into ¹/₄ in (7 mm) thick. Set aside to drain.

2. Cut green onion into ¹/₂ in (1.5 cm) pieces.

3. Heat 2 T oil in wok; add green onion and gingerroot. Stir fry for 1 minute over high heat. Discard green onion and gingerroot.

4. Turn down heat to medium and add oyster sauce, soy sauce, *sake*, chicken stock and *tofu*; stir well. Add mushrooms and sprinkle pepper and cook for 5 minutes over medium heat.

5. Add mixed vegetables and bring to a boil. Add cornstarch mixture; stir well until thickened. Remove from heat.

This Sweet & Sour Sauce recipe can be used for fish and meat dishes, also.

INGREDIENTS: 4 servings

4 deep-fried *tofu* cutlets (*atsuage*) or HOMEMADE DEEP-FRIED *TOFU* CUTLETS (see page 57)
1³/4 oz (50 g) bamboo shoots, cut into 2 in (5 cm) long julienne strips, about ¹/2 C
1 carrot, cut into 2 in (5 cm) long julienne strips
2 green peppers sliced thin
4 *shiitake* mushrooms or 8 fresh mushrooms
1 zucchini, ¹/4 in (0.7 cm) thick slices
1 C bean sprouts
3–4 T vegetable oil
Sweet & Sour Sauce
4 T rice vinegar
2 T light soy sauce
1¹/2 T sugar
2 T ketchup
1¹/4 C chicken broth
1 T cornstarch plus 2 T water for thickening

1. Dip deep-fried *tofu* into boiling water for 30 seconds to remove grease; drain on paper towels. Cut into triangles or serving sizes.

2. Soak *shiitake* mushrooms in lukewarm water until soft; cut off stems. Slice thin.

3. Mix all **Sweet & Sour Sauce** ingredients. Set aside.

4. Heat wok over medium-high heat; add 2 T oil. Add bamboo shoots, carrot, green peppers, mushrooms, zucchini and bean sprouts and stir for 2 to 3 minutes.

5. Blend in **Sweet & Sour Sauce** ingredients and cook for 2 minutes over high heat. Add dissolved cornstarch and boil 30 seconds. Remove from heat.

6. Heat 2 T oil in 12-inch skillet over medium-high heat; add *tofu* cutlets; stir fry for 1 minute. Place in serving platter and serve **Sweet & Sour Sauce** over *tofu* cutlets.

HOMEMADE *TOFU* CUTLETS

4 firm *tofu*, well drained, about
    12 oz (300g) each
Oil for deep-frying (375°F/175°)

Remove excess surface moisture from firm *tofu*. Heat oil in a wok or deep-fryer to 375°F (190°C). Slide in *tofu* carefully; deep-fry 3 to 3½ minutes, stir occasionally until crisp and golden brown. Drain on a wire rack.

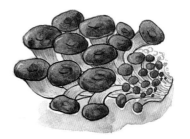

OKARA AND VEGETABLE CUTLETS

A {
6¹/₂ oz (185g) or 1¹/₂ C *okara*
1 C all-purpose flour, sifted
2 T onion, chopped
2 T carrot, chopped
2 T zucchini, chopped
1 T celery, chopped
1 egg, beaten
1¹/₂ T light soy sauce
¹/₄ t dry Chinese mustard powder
1 T curry powder
¹/₂ t salt
}

All purpose flour for coating
2 eggs, beaten
Panko (dehydrated bread crumbs) for coating
Oil for deep-frying
Condiments
Equal amounts of ketchup & Worcestershire sauce
Garnishes
Lemon wedges
Parsley

These cutlets can be served as a vegetarian main dish and are guaranteed to win applause.

1. Mix all ingredients **A**; divide into eighths. Form oval patties.

2. Coat patties with flour, beaten eggs and bread crumbs as shown.

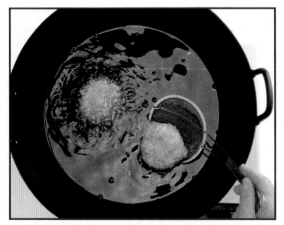

3. Deep-fry in 340–360°F (170–180°C) oil until golden brown. Drain on wire rack.

OKARA WITH SCRAMBLED EGGS AND VEGETABLES

INGREDIENTS: 4 servings

Microwave cooking
1½-quart glass casserole dish

3 C (about 14 oz/400 g) *okara*
1 deep-fried *tofu* pouch (*aburaage*)
3 T vegetable oil
⅓ C carrot, shredded
½ C bamboo shoots, shredded
   (about 1¾ oz/50 g)
2 eggs, beaten
10 pea pods or 2 T green peas
A { ½ T *dashi* stock
{ 4 T *mirin* or sugar
{ 4½ T light soy sauce

A quick method of cooking *okara* makes this dish a nutritious and hearty side dish to serve with hurry-up suppers.

1. Line glass baking dish with 2 thicknesses of paper towel. Place deep-fried *tofu* pouch on top; cover with another paper towel to avoid spattering.
2. Cook on full power for 30 seconds. Cut into thin slices.

3. In glass dish, combine *okara* and vegetable oil; cover with plastic wrap and cook on full power for 3 minutes, stir 1–2 times during cooking.

7. Trim pea pods, and wrap with plastic wrap; cook on full power for 20 seconds. Slice thin.
8. Mix *okara* with deep-fried *tofu* pouch and pea pods.

4. Add carrot and bamboo shoots; cover and cook on full power for 3 minutes.

5. Add ingredients **A**; cover and cook on full power for 4 minutes.

6. Add beaten eggs; mix well and cook on full power for 1 to 2 minutes. ↗

59

NATTO AND *SHIMEJI* MUSHROOM SPAGHETTI SAUCE

INGREDIENTS: 4 servings

4 1³/₄ oz (50 g) each package *natto* (or 2 3¹/₂ oz/100 g each *natto*)

1 T soy sauce

2 t Chinese mustard*

1 t garlic, finely chopped

3 oz (85 g) *shimeji* mushrooms

1 17 oz (482 g) can whole corn, drained

8 oz (225 g) uncooked spaghetti

1 T vegetable oil

1 T (¹/₈ stick) butter or margarine

4 T green onion, chopped

1 large sheet (8¹/₄ × 7¹/₄ in/21 ×18 cm) *nori* seaweed, crumbled

4 T Parmesan cheese

*Mix 1 T water to 1 T dry powder

This enchanting combination of spaghetti and *natto* with *shimeji* mushrooms adds interest to the most routine spaghetti sauce.

3. Cook spaghetti as directed on package; drain. Toss with 1 T butter. Keep warm.

1. Chop *natto* into small pieces; mix with soy sauce and mustard. Set aside.

2. Discard hard stem ends of mushrooms; separate to small pieces. ↗

7. Serve *natto-shimeji* mushroom sauce over spaghetti; sprinkle with chopped green onion, *nori* seaweed and Parmesan cheese.

4. Heat 1 T oil in 12 in skillet; sauté garlic and mushrooms until soft over medium-high heat.

5. Add corn and mix well. Heat to boiling. Remove from heat.

6. Stir in *natto*; fluff mixture lightly with fork. ↗

BOILED SOYBEANS WITH KELP

INGREDIENTS: 4 servings

1 C dried soybeans
1 4 in (10 cm) square kelp (*kombu*)
4 C water
1/2 C sugar
7 T *sake*
3 1/2 T soy sauce

Soybeans are high in vegetable protein. Combing them with kelp makes a nourishing side dish for any meal.

1. Clean soybeans and soak them in water several hours or overnight.
2. In a Dutch oven or 3-quart saucepan, pour 5 C water and softened soybeans. Bring to a boil. Turn heat to moderate and cover and simmer until beans are almost tender, about 1 hour. Skim scum if necessary.

3. Wipe off white powder from kelp. Cut into 1/4 in (7 mm) square pieces.

4. Add to beans. Add sugar and *sake*; simmer over low heat until most of liquid is gone.
5. Add soy sauce; remove from heat; cover and let stand 5 minutes.

NOTE: If you can't find soybeans, use another variety; they are interchangeable. You can expect the beans to double or triple in volume as they cook.

If you have leftover kelp from *dashi* stock, use that piece in this recipe.

TOFU AND CUCUMBER SALAD

INGREDIENTS: 4 servings

1 14 oz (400 g) cube firm *tofu,*
well drained

Sweet & Sour Dressing
- 3 T rice vinegar
- 2¹/₂ T sugar
- ¹/₂ T light soy sauce
- 1 t salt
- ¹/₂ t sesame oil

2 or 3 Japanese cucumbers

Hot Bean Sauce
- ¹/₂ t hot bean paste
- ²/₃ t salt
- 2 t sesame oil

1 T toasted sesame seeds (see
page 100)

Crisp cucumbers and soft *tofu* texture blend well with zesty dressing.

1. Cook *tofu* in 3-quart saucepan filled with boiling water for 1 minute. Cut into ¹/₂ in (1.5 cm) cubes.

2. Mix all **Sweet & Sour Dressing.** Toss *tofu* with dresssing; refrigerate for 30 minutes or longer.

3. Cut cucumbers into halves lengthwise. Cut each piece into fourths crosswise (about 1³/₄ in/4.5 cm).

4. Mix all **Hot Bean Sauce** ingredients; toss with cucumber.

5. Mix chilled *tofu* and cucumber. Sprinkle sesame seeds on top.

CUCUMBER AND SHRIMP ROLLS

This colorful chilled *tofu* salad can be served with an elegant party dish.

INGREDIENTS: 4 servings

2 14 oz (400g) cube firm *tofu*, well drained
¼ small cucumber, cut into julienne strips
2 oz (60g) cocktail shrimp
5 thin sliced fresh gingerroot
2 *shiso* leaves
Garnishes
Lemon peel
Chinese mustard
Condiment
Soy sauce

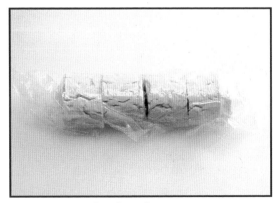

1. Cut sliced gingerroot into julienne strips; soak in water.
2. Cut *shiso* leaves into thin slices.
3. Slice *tofu* crosswise into fourths.
4. Place plastic wrap on a bamboo mat.
5. Place *tofu* pieces, one-half portion of cucumber, shrimp, drained gingerroot and *shiso* leaves as shown.

6. Roll up. Repeat for other *tofu*.
7. Refrigerate for ½ to 1 hour.
8. Slice into fourths.

TOFU RING WITH TUNA SALAD

Ordinary tuna salad turns into refreshing texture and flavor with *tofu* mayonnaise.

Makes 7 in (18 cm) × 2 in (5 cm) ring mold

Tofu Ring
7 oz (200 g) firm *tofu*
2 T unflavored gelatine
3¹/₂ T water
²/₃ C chicken broth
¹/₃ C tomato juice
¹/₈ t each salt & pepper
1 hard boiled egg

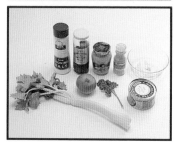

Tuna Salad
1 can (6¹/₂ oz/184 g) tuna, drained
1 T parsley, minced
1 T dill pickles, chopped
1 T onion, chopped
1 T celery, diced
2 T *TOFU* MAYONNAISE (see page 67)
1 T Dijon mustard
¹/₈ t each salt & pepper

Garnishes
Horseradish sprouts or alfalfa sprouts
Lemon slices

1. Heat 2 C water to boiling in 2-quart saucepan; add *tofu*. Heat to boiling. Drain *tofu*; cut into $^1/_2$ in (1.5 cm) cubes; refrigerate for 30 minutes or longer.

2. Mix gelatine and $3^1/_2$ T of water in a small saucepan. Stir over low heat until mixture is hot.

3. Pour into a bowl and stir in remaining chicken broth, tomato juice, salt & pepper. Chill until slightly thickened and syrupy.

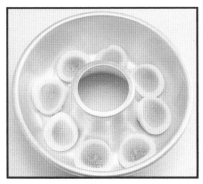

4. Place sliced egg and chilled *tofu* cubes into lightly oiled metal ring; pour gelatine mixture in the ring. Chill until firm, several hours or overnight.

5. Place a serving platter on top of mold, then invert and unmold.
6. Fill center with **tuna salad.** Garnish with horseradish sprouts and lemon slices.

TUNA SALAD

For salad, mix tuna with parsley, pickles, onion, celery, *TOFU* **MAYONNAISE,** mustard, salt & pepper. Chill (2–3 hours).

When ready to serve, dip mold into lukewarm water for a few seconds, run knife around the edge, and then tap to loosen.

NOTE: Potato or macaroni salad can be substituted for tuna salad.

TOFU TEMPURA SALAD

This salad can be served as a delightful vegetarian dish.

INGREDIENTS: 4 servings

21 oz (600 g) *TOFU TEMPURA* (see page 23)
2 tomatoes, cut into wedges
4 C shredded cabbage
¹/₂ carrot, shredded
2 T raisins, softend in water
1 lemon, cut into wedges
3 or 4 radishes

Salad dressing
¹/₃ C rice vinegar or wine vinegar
²/₃ C vegetable oil
1 t salt
¹/₄ t pepper

1. Mix cabbage, carrot and raisins together.
2. Place *tempura* in salad plate or bowl, arrange cabbage and carrot mixture around *tofu*. Place tomatoes and lemon wedges.

3. Pour salad dressing just before serving.

TOFU MAYONNAISE

A combination of *tofu* and *miso* is a welcome contribution to a low-calorie, high-protein dressing.

INGREDIENTS: Makes ³/₄ cup

7 oz (200 g) firm *tofu*
7 T vegetable oil
3 T rice vinegar
2 T lemon juice
2 t (heaping) red *miso*
1–1¹/₂ t salt
¹/₈ t white pepper

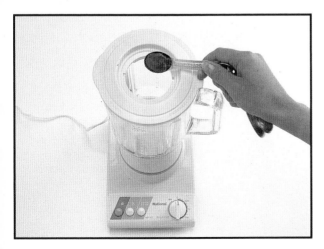

Combine all ingredients in a blender; beat until smooth, 30 to 40 seconds. Cover and refrigerate about 2 hours or overnight.

NOTE: *TOFU* **MAYONNAISE** keeps for up to one week in a refrigerator.

GRILLED *TOFU* AND VEGETABLE SALAD

Tofu mayonnaise and a touch of toasted sesame seeds provide the distinctive flavor to this salad.

INGREDIENTS: 4 servings

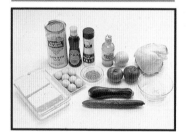

2 cubes (10^1/$_2$ oz, 300g each) firm *tofu*, well drained
1 T vegetable oil
^{1}/$_2$ t sesame oil
^{3}/$_4$ C *TOFU* MAYONNAISE (see page 67)
8 fresh mushrooms, sliced
Lettuce
2 medium tomatoes, cut into ^{1}/$_2$ inch pieces
1 medium cucumber or zucchini, thinly sliced
^{1}/$_2$ T lemon juice
1 T toasted sesame seeds (see page 100)
^{1}/$_4$ t salt

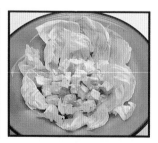

1. Cut *tofu* crosswise into halves.
2. Heat vegetable oil and sesame oil in 12 in skillet and grill *tofu* pieces on both sides until golden brown. Let it cool and cover and refrigerate about 1 hour.

3. Sprinkle lemon juice onto mushroom slices.
4. Tear lettuce into bite-size pieces. Set aside.
5. Toss mushrooms, tomatoes, cucumbers with 2 T *TOFU* **MAYONNAISE**.

6. Cut chilled *tofu* into ^{3}/$_4$ in (2 cm) cubes; toss with 2 T *TOFU* **MAYONNAISE**.
7. Place *tofu* into salad bowl.

8. Place vegetable mixture around *tofu*; sprinkle toasted sesame seeds and salt on top. Serve with additional mayonnaise dresssing, if you desire.

CHICKEN SALAD WITH *TOFU* MAYONNAISE

3/4 C *TOFU* MAYONNAISE (see page 67)
2 chicken breasts, skinned and boned (about 1 pound)
1 T wine
1/2 t salt
1 carrot, shredded
1 cucumber, sliced
Paprika (optional)
Salad greens

Chicken salad will never seem the same after you have tried this delicious *tofu* mayonnaise.

Microwave cooking

1. Sprinkle wine and salt on chicken breasts.
2. Arrange chicken in glass baking dish; cover with wax paper.
3. Cook on full power for 4 to 5 minutes. Turn pieces over and continue to cook 3 minutes. Allow to stand 5 minutes. Let chicken breasts cool and chill in a refrigerator for 30 minutes.

4. Toss carrot and cucumber with 2 T *TOFU* **MAYONNAISE**.

5. Shred chicken breasts; toss with 2 T *TOFU* **MAYONNAISE**. Set aside.
6. Place on salad greens; sprinkle paprika, if desire. Serve with *TOFU* **MAYONNAISE**.

NOTE: Leftover roasted chicken can be substituted for the chicken breasts.

FRUIT SALAD DRESSING

This quick recipe will be nice with any fresh fruits.

12 oz (340g) soft *tofu,* well drained
¹/₂ T lemon juice
¹/₃ C chilled half-and-half
¹/₂ t salt
1¹/₂ T sugar
1 T honey
¹/₄ t vanilla extract

2–3 C assorted fresh fruit*

*Oranges, kiwi fruits, strawberries, bananas, peaches, pineapples, avocados, apples

Combine all ingredients in blender; beat until smooth, 45 to 50 seconds.

PARTY DIP

A delicately flavored *tofu* dip with yogurt and the familiar presence of cream cheese provides an unusual, yet nourishing texture.

INGREDIENTS: Makes 1¹/₂ cups

14 oz (400g) firm *tofu,* well drained
3 oz (85g) cream cheese
²/₃ C plain yogurt
¹/₂ t salt
¹/₈ t white pepper
1 T Parmesan cheese

1 T minced parsley

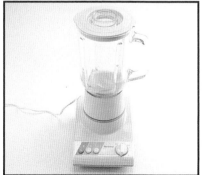

1. Combine all ingredients except parsley in blender; beat until smooth, 30 to 40 seconds.
2. Mix with minced parsley.
3. Serve dip with crackers, potato chips, carrot sticks, celery sticks or radishes.

SALMON QUICHE

The savory ingredients enhance the flavor of salmon. This elegant dish can be served hot or cold.

INGREDIENTS: Makes 1 9 in (23 cm) pie

Microwave cooking or regular oven cooking

$10^1/_2$–12 oz (300–340 g) firm *tofu*, well drained
2 cans ($7^3/_4$ oz, 220 g each) salmon or cooked salmon fillet
$^2/_3$ C chopped spinach leaves
2 T minced parsley
1 9 in (23 cm) baked pie shell (see page 73)
1 C grated Cheddar cheese
3 eggs, lightly beaten
$^2/_3$ C milk
2 T onion, chopped
$^1/_2$ t salt

Microwave cooking

1. In a medium bowl, combine *tofu*, salmon; beat until smooth.

2. Add spinach and parsley and mix well; add ¹/₂ C Cheddar cheese.

3. Combine eggs, milk, salt and chopped onion; mix well.

4. Mix with salmon mixture.

5. Place mixture in baked pastry shell. Sprinkle ¹/₂ C of Cheddar cheese on top.

6. Cook on full power for 12 to 15 minutes, turn dish twice during cooking. Let sit for 10 minutes or until center is firm.

Oven cooking

Bake in pre-heated oven, 325°F (163°C), for 40 to 45 minutes.

Pie Shell

INGREDIENTS: Makes 1 9 in (23 cm) shell

1¹/₂ C all-purpose flour, sifted
1¹/₄ t salt
¹/₂ C vegetable oil
3 t milk

1. Mix flour and salt.
2. Mix oil and milk; add to flour.
3. Mix and knead.
4. Shape dough into a flattened round with rolling pin.
5. Place in pie dish. Prick the pie shell all over with a fork so that air trapped below the shell can escape rather than cause bubbles in the crust.
6. Bake in 475°F (245°C) oven for 5 to 7 minutes. Let it cool

TOFU OMELET

When planning a party breakfast or brunch, surprise your guests with the colorful *tofu* fillings.

INGREDIENTS: 1 serving

4 oz (115 g) firm *tofu*, well drained
1/8 t each salt & pepper
2 eggs, lightly beaten

1/2 small tomato, chopped
1 T green pepper, chopped
1 T butter or margarine
Condiments
Ketchup
Soy sauce

1. Crumble *tofu* and season with salt and pepper.

2. Melt butter in skillet over medium high heat; pour in eggs.

3. Cook until eggs are bubbly; add *tofu*, tomato and green pepper on top.

4. Fold into three.

STEAMED *TOFU* AND EGGS (*Kuyamushi*)

INGREDIENTS: 4 servings

**4³/₄ in (12 cm) diameter &
2¹/₂ in (6.5 cm) deep bowl**

14 oz (400 g) soft or firm *tofu*
¹/₂ t salt
4 small *shiitake* mushrooms,
   soften in ¹/₂ C of water,
   reserve soaking liquid
8 pea pods, cooked
2 T frozen green peas
1 T chopped green onion

A {
2 large eggs, beaten
1¹/₂ C *dashi* stock
1 t light soy sauce
²/₃ t salt
1 t *mirin*
}

B {
Shiitake soaking liquid
   (about 9 T)
1 t light soy sauce
1 T sugar
}

Garnishes
Yuzu citron, lime peels
Coriander

Creamy soft *tofu* with eggs is delicately flavored with soy sauce. Sprinkle with *yuzu* citron peel.

1. Cut *tofu* into fourths; Cook in boiling water with ¹/₂ t salt for 1 minute; drain.

2. Place in individual steaming bowl.

3. Trim hard stem ends from *shiitake* mushrooms and cut in halves; cook in ingredients **B** for 5 minutes over medium heat.

4. Mix ingredients **A** together.

5. Place *shiitake* and frozen peas in each bowl.
6. Pour egg mixture in.

7. Place bowls in steamer and cover with wax paper; steam for 5 minutes over high heat and turn heat to medium and steam another 12 to 15 minutes.

8. Sprinkle green onion if you desire and arrange cooked pea pods on top.

NOTE: Chicken breast or shrimp can be added to this dish with *tofu*.

RICE GRUEL WITH EGG AND *TOFU*

RICE GRUEL (*Shiragayu*

This nourishing dish can be served as a protein rich supplement to meat dishes.

2¹/₂–3 C cooked rice gruel
2 t salt
¹/₂ t light soy sauce
6–7 oz (170–200 g) soft or firm *tofu*, cut into ¹/₂ in (1.5 cm) cubes
1 C chopped spinach or *mitsuba*, trefoil
2 eggs, beaten

1. Prepare rice gruel as directed below, in saucepan; add salt, and light soy sauce. Stir gently and add *tofu* cubes.

2. Cook over medium heat until it boils; add chopped spinach and beaten eggs.
3. Turn off heat and cover. Leave on stove 2 to 3 minutes.

RICE GRUEL (*Shiragayu*)

¹/₂ C short grain rice (Japanese-type rice)
2¹/₂ C water

1. Wash rice by rubbing between hands. Drain until water is clear; drain well in a basket.
2. In 3-quart saucepan, add water and rice; cook until it boils over high heat without lid on.
3. Turn heat to low and continue cooking for 40 to 50 minutes. Add boiling water if necessary during cooking.

NOTE: Leftover rice can be used for gruel rice.

2 C cold cooked rice
5 C *dashi* stock or water
Ingredients other than rice are sauce as those given in RICE

1. Wash rice in wire basket until most of starch is removed. Drain.
2. In 3-quart saucepan, mix *dashi* stock or water with salt and soy sauce; bring to a boil over high heat.
3. Add rinsed rice; bring to a boil over medium heat. Add *tofu*, spinach and beaten eggs.
4. Simmer for 2 to 3 minutes over low heat with lid on.

NOODLES AND OYSTERS WITH *MISO* SOUP

10$\frac{1}{2}$–14 oz (300–400 g) soft or
firm *tofu*
14 oz (400 g) oysters
1 bunch green onion
8 oz (225 g) uncooked noodles

***Miso* Soup**
⎰ 5 C *dashi* stock
⎱ 10 level T white *miso*
⎰ 2 T *mirin*

Garnishes
Yuzu citron
Lemon or lime
7-spice powder (*shichimi-togarashi*)

Miso soup provides a rich, full bodied flavor to this Japanese interpretation of the oyster stew.

1. Cut *tofu* into 1 in (2.5 cm) cubes.
2. Rinse oysters in salted water and drain.
3. Cut green onion into diagonal slices.

4. Bring some water to a boil in large saucepan and cook noodles until tender. Rinse, drain and place in noodle bowls.

5. In medium size saucepan, heat *dashi* stock over high heat until it boils; add *miso* and *mirin*, and stir well.
6. Add *tofu* and green onion and bring to a boil.
7. Add oysters and reduce heat to medium; cook for 2 to 3 minutes. Be careful not to overcook oysters. Place oysters, *tofu* and green onion on noodles. Pour *miso* soup over noodles.

DEEP-FRIED *TOFU* POUCHES ON RICE

This low-calorie, high-protein dish is ideal for lunch.

INGREDIENTS: 2 servings

2 deep-fried *tofu* pouches (*aburaage*)
1 medium onion, sliced and separated into rings
2 green onion stalks, cut into 1 in (2.5 cm) diagonal slices
1 can (4 oz/115 g) sliced mushrooms, drained
Dash of salt & pepper
2 eggs, lightly beaten
2 cups hot cooked rice (see page 93)
Cooking Broth
⎰ 1 C *dashi* stock
⎱ ¼ C *mirin*
⎰ 1 t light soy sauce
⎱ 2½ t low salt soy sauce

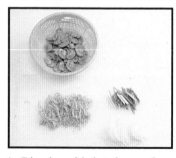

1. Dip deep-fried *tofu* pouches into boiling water for 1 minute to remove excess grease. Drain on paper towels and slice thin.

2. In 12 in (30 cm) skillet, heat cooking broth over medium-high heat and add *tofu* pouches and onion. Cook until onion is soft; add green onion and mushrooms; bring to a boil. Sprinkle salt & pepper.

3. Pour over beaten eggs; cook until eggs are half cooked over medium-high heat.
4. Place cooked hot rice in bowls; place half portion of cooked ingredients on top. Pour over broth.

STEAMED RICE WITH DEEP-FRIED *TOFU* POUCHES

2¹/₂ short grain Japanese type rice

A {
3 C water or chicken broth
2 T *sake*
1 T soy sauce
1 t *mirin*
1 t salt
}

2 *shiitake* mushrooms, softened in water

3¹/₂ oz (100g) chicken breast, skinned and boned

B {
1 t *sake*
1 t soy sauce
}

2 deep-fried *tofu* pouches (*aburaage*)

¹/₄ C pea pods, cooked and sliced thin

This is a delicately flavored steamed rice with deep-fried *tofu* pouches laced with soy sauce and *sake*, and the presence of *shimeji* mushrooms and chicken provides a nourishing texture.

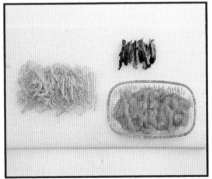

1. Wash, rinse and drain rice; leave for 30 to 45 minutes.
2. Slice *shiitake* mushrooms. Cut chicken breast into small pieces and marinate in ingredients **B**.
3. Boil *tofu* pouches in water for 30 seconds; drain on paper towels. Slice into thin pieces.

4. In Dutch oven or electric rice cooker, mix rice, *tofu* pouches and ingredients **A**. Add chicken and *shiitake* mushrooms.
5. Cook for 20 minutes over medium high heat, when using Dutch oven.
6. Let it steam for ten minutes. Toss in cooked pea pods.

DEEP-FRIED *TOFU* POUCH *SUSHI* (*Inari-zushi*)

Japan's one of all-time favorites is good for brunch or picnic.

INGREDIENTS: Makes 20

3³/₄–4 C prepared *sushi* rice (see page 93)
10 deep-fried *tofu* pouches (*aburaage*)
1²/₃ C *dashi* stock

A { ¹/₂ C sugar
      3 t *mirin*
      4 T soy sauce

²/₃ oz (20g) dried gourd strips (*kanpyo*)

B { ¹/₃ C *dashi* stock
      3 T sugar
      3 T soy sauce

4 dried *shiitake* mushrooms, softened. Reserve soaking liquid
1 carrot, shredded

C { ¹/₃ C *dashi* stock
      ¹/₃ C *shiitake* soaking liquid
      2 T *mirin*
      1¹/₂ T soy sauce
      1 T *sake*

1 Japanese cucumber

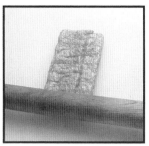

1. Press *tofu* pouches with rolling pin for easy opening.

2. Cut in half.

3. Open with thumbs.

4. In a large saucepan, heat water to a boil; add *tofu* pouches and cook for 2 minutes to remove excess grease. Drain on paper towels.

5. Heat cooking sauce **A** in 3-quart saucepan over medium heat; add *tofu* pouches and cook for 20 minutes or until most of the liquid is absorbed. Allow to cool.

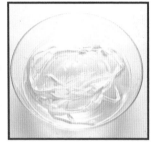

6. Soak dried gourd strips in water until soft.

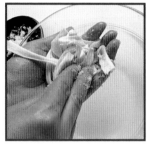

7. Wash in salted water and rinse well.

8. In medium saucepan, add 2¹/₂ C water and softened gourd strips; cook for 15 minutes over medium heat. Drain.

9. In medium saucepan heat cooking sauce **B**; add gourd strips. Cook over medium heat for 20 minutes. Allow to cool.

10. Cut into ¹/₄ in (0.7 cm) squares. Set aside.

11. Trim hard stem ends of *shiitake* mushrooms. Cut into ¹/₄ in (0.7 cm) cubes. Chop carrot.

12. Cook *shiitake* mushrooms and carrot in cooking sauce **C.**

13. Wash cucumber; slice thin and chop. Soak in salted water (1 T salt) for 5 minutes. Drain and squeeze well.

14. Mix cooked vegetables and cucumber with prepared *sushi* rice. Mix well. Fill *tofu* pouches using a spoon.

TOFU CHEESE CAKE

Okara pie shell makes this cheese cake truly unique.

INGREDIENTS: Makes 1 9 in (23 cm) pie

2 T gelatine, unflavored
$^2/_3$ C water
$^1/_4$ C sugar
12 oz (340 g) firm *tofu*, well drained
10 oz (285 g) plain yogurt
$3^1/_2$ oz (100 g) cream cheese

1 baked 9 in (23 cm) pie shell (see page 83)

Toppings
Fresh kiwi fruits, strawberries, bananas or oranges
Canned pie fillings-blueberry or cherry

1. Empty two envelopes of gelatine into $^2/_3$ C of water; stir and leave for 10 minutes.

2. Dissolve gelatine mixture over low heat, stirring constantly.

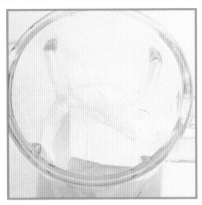

3. Beat sugar, *tofu*, plain yogurt and cream cheese until smooth.

4. Pour dissolved gelatine into cream cheese mixture and beat for 30 seconds.

5. Pour into baked pie shell. Chill until firm, or refrigerate over night. ↗

6. Arrange fruit slices on top. Cut into wedges to serve.

Okara Pie Shell

INGREDIENTS: Makes 1 9 in (23 cm) pie

1 C *okara*, packed
2$^1/_2$ oz (70 g) almonds, toasted
4 T butter or margarine
$^1/_8$ t vanilla extract

Microwave method

1. Place *okara* in 9–10 in (23–25.5 cm) pie plate.
2. Cover with plastic wrap. Cook on full power for 5 minutes. Stir.
3. Cook another 5 minutes, uncovered. Stir and cook another 3 minutes.
4. Mix *okara* with toasted and crumbled almonds. Set aside.
5. In a glass pie plate, cook butter on full power for 30 seconds or until melted. Add vanilla extract.
6. Stir *okara* into butter until well blended.
7. Press mixture firmly against bottom and sides of the pie plate.
8. Cook on full power for 2$^1/_2$ to 3 minutes. Let it cool.

BANANA PUDDING PIE

When serving this pie or pudding, dress it up by garnishing with sliced banana.

INGREDIENTS: Makes 1 9 in (23 cm) pie

1 T unflavored gelatine
$^1/_3$ C water

A $\begin{cases} \text{10}^1/_2 \text{ oz (300 g) firm } tofu, \text{ well drained} \\ \text{1 large egg} \\ \text{3 T sugar} \\ \text{2 T honey} \\ \text{2 T lemon juice} \\ \text{2 bananas} \\ \text{A dash of cinnamon powder} \end{cases}$

1 9 in (23 cm) crumb pie crust (see page 85)

Topping
$^1/_2$ banana
Dash of lemon juice
Touch of cinnamon powder
1 cherry (optional) or strawberries

1. Empty an envelope of gelatine into $^1/_3$ C of water; stir and leave for 5 minutes.

2. Cook gelatine over low heat until dissolved.

3. Mix ingredients **A** and beat until smooth.

6. Slice banana and sprinkle lemon juice. Arrange banana slices and cherry or strawberries on top.
7. Sprinkle cinnamon powder.

4. Pour gelatine into *tofu* mixture and beat a few seconds.

5. Pour into prepared pie shell. Cover with wax paper and refrigerate until firm, about 3 hours. ↗

Graham Cracker Pie Crust

INGREDIENTS: Makes 1 9 in (23 cm) pie

1 pack Graham crackers, finely rolled (about 1$^2/_3$ C crumbs)
$^1/_3$ C softened butter or margarine

1. Blend crumbs and butter well with fork or pastry blender.
2. Using back of large spoon, press crumb mixture inside 9 inch pie plate to coat bottom and sides evenly.
3. Chill in refrigerator 30 minutes before using.

OKARA PANCAKE

Keep this easy recipe in mind the next time you have extra *okara*.

$^{1}/_{2}$ C *okara*, packed (2 oz/60 g)
1 C all-purpose flour
1 C sugar
2 large eggs
$^{1}/_{2}$ t soda
1 t water

4 T water

$^{1}/_{2}$ t vanilla extract
4 T butter or margarine
Pancake syrup or honey
$4^{1}/_{4}$ oz (120 g) ready-made bean paste (optional)

4–6 T vegetable oil

1. Toast *okara* (page 87).
2. Sift flour and sugar.
3. Beat eggs and sugar until stiff peaks form.
4. Mix soda with 1 t water; add to egg and sugar mixture.
5. Add 2 T water and mix with *okara* and flour. Leave for 30 minutes.
6. Add 2 T water and stir well.
7. Heat a skillet, pour thin film of oil; pour about 3 T of batter to form 3 in (7.5 cm) pancake; cook over low to medium heat ↗ until surface becomes bubbly. Turn and fry until lightly brown.
8. Serve with butter, syrup or honey while hot.

NOTE: For your snack, place some bean paste between two pieces of pancakes.

OKARA COOKIES

INGREDIENTS: Makes 60 (1¹/₄ in/3 cm) round or 32 (2 in/5 cm) round cookies

2 C *okara*, dried*
1¹/₃ C oatmeal
¹/₂ C sesame seeds, toasted
1¹/₂ C all-purpose flour
1¹/₃ t baking soda
¹/₂ C plus 2 T margarine
¹/₂ C plus 2 T shortening
³/₄ C sugar
2 eggs, beaten
2 t lemon juice
¹/₄ C raisins (optional)

*8 oz (225 g) *okara* makes 2 C after dried.

Preheat oven to 400°F (205°C)

These cookies can be preserved well in an air-tight container and serve as a nourishing breakfast or snack.

1. Remove moisture from *okara**.

2. Crush oatmeal and mix with sesame seeds. Set aside.
3. Sift flour and baking soda twice; add oatmeal and sesame seeds.
4. Sift sugar. Mix margarine and shortening; add sugar. Whip it until mixture gets white.

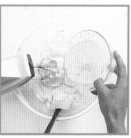

5. Add beaten eggs and lemon juice.

6. Add flour, baking soda, oatmeal & sesame seed mixture, *okara* and raisins.

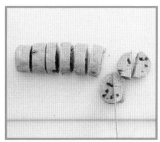

7. Knead and roll. Make 2 (2 in/5 cm in diameter) logs. If dough is soft, keep in refrigerator for 30 minutes.

8. Divide each log into 16 pieces. Make 2 in (5 cm) round cookies. Bake in preheated oven at 400°F (205°C) for 20 to 25 minutes.

Removing moisture from *okara*

Microwave oven method
1. Spread *okara* on a plate.
2. Cover with plastic wrap and cook on full power for 5 minutes. Stir.
3. Cook another 5 minutes, uncover.
4. Turn and stir, cook another 3 minutes.
Oven method
1. Spread *okara* on a baking dish.
2. Dry *okara* in the oven for 10 minutes at 300–325°F (150–163°C).
3. Stir and dry another 5 minutes.
Skillet method
1. Toast *okara* in a skillet for 20 minutes over low heat.

SOYMILK AND *TOFU* SHAKE

PEACH AND
SOYMILK SHAKE

TOFU AND
PINEAPPLE SHAKE

SOYMILK

COFFEE FLAVORED
SOYMILK

Soymilk can be served at breakfast time or at any other meal.

SOYMILK

INGREDIENTS: Makes 2 cups

5¹/₄ oz (150g) soybeans (³/₄ C)
2¹/₂ C water
3 T honey
3 drops vanilla extract
2¹/₂ C ice water

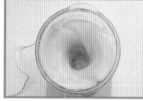

1. Soak soybeans in 2¹/₂ C of water overnight. Increases in volume 2.3 times.

2. In a blender, mix 2¹/₂ C ice water and softened soybeans; beat for 1 minute or until smooth.

3. In a 3-quart saucepan, pour soybean mixture and cook for 10 minutes over medium heat, stir constantly.

4. Strain the soymilk with pastry cloth while hot.

5. Add honey and vanilla extract.

NOTE: It keeps for a day or two in a refrigerator.

TOFU AND PINEAPPLE SHAKE

INGREDIENTS: Makes 4 cups

10¹/₂-12 oz (300-340g) soft *tofu*, well drained
1 C crushed pineapple with juice
1 banana
¹/₂ C low fat milk or soymilk
1-2 C crushed ice
3 T honey
3 drops vanilla extract
Cinnamon powder (optional)

Combine all ingredients in blender; beat until smooth, 45 seconds.

88

PEACH AND SOYMILK SHAKE

INGREDIENTS: Makes 4 cups

1¹/₂ C soymilk
1 can (14³/₄ oz/420g) peach halves, with syrup
¹/₂ T lemon juice
2 T honey
6 ice cubes
¹/₈ t vanilla extract

1. Cut peaches into 1 in (2.5cm) cubes.
2. Combine all ingredients in a blender; beat 1 minute.

NOTE: Fresh papaya or strawberries can be used if preferred.

COFFEE FLAVORED SOYMILK

INGREDIENTS: Makes about 2 cups

2-2¹/₂ C soymilk
1¹/₂ T instant coffee powder
3-4 T honey
6-8 ice cubes

Combine all ingredients in a blender; beat until smooth, 30 seconds.

INFORMATION

MENU PLANNING

Basic Rules

1. Seasonal appropriateness

Special attention should be given to the ingredients you choose. Some fresh fish and vegetables are available only at certain times of a year. Therefore, consider using seasonal ingredients which are abundant in the market.

2. Occasion

To serve a Japanese meal does not have to be so tedious. There are many one-pot dishes cooked on the table.

Consider the number of people you serve and whether you serve for festive occasions, luncheon, dinner, picnic or etc.

3. Flavor and Texture

Plan your menu with meat, fish and vegetables. Make each dish with different cooking method, such as grilled, steamed, fried, etc.

4. Color

Presentation of food is also important. Each ingredient has different flavor, texture and color. It is important to appeal to the eyes as well as to the tongue.

5. Nutrition

It helps when determining the kind of food to serve according to the diners' physical conditions and ages.

6. Cost

Seasonal fresh items generally mark lower prices. See the weekly specials for your menu planning.

Preparation

Step I

1. Read recipes carefully and thoroughly.
2. Write down all necessary ingredients you need to buy.
3. Check all cooking equipment and place within reach.
4. Arrange all necessary seasonings, spices and herbs on kitchen counter or within your reach.
5. Prepare measuring cups and spoons.
6. Prepare all serving bowls, plates and platters near you. You may need to keep some serving platters warm.

Step II

1. Put comfortable clothes on and wear an apron, so that you will be psychologically ready for cooking.
2. Prepare plenty of kitchen towels and paper towels.

Step III

Hot food should be placed on warmed plate and cold food on chilled plate. Also look at the design on the plate if any before you place food on it. Place the plate so that the design faces the diner. With towel, wipe off around the rim if there are spilled bits or traces of liquid.

PREPARATION

HOMEMADE *TOFU*

Makes 1 cube (10½–14 oz/300–400 g) *tofu*

10½ oz (300 g) soybeans, washed, rinsed and drained
5 C water
1 package 1¼ oz (35 g) *nigari** or 5½ T liquid solidifier

      *Obtain the solidifier from a *tofu* shop, natural food store, Japanese food market, or chemical supply house in your area.

1. In a large bowl, soak soybeans in 5 C of water for several hours or overnight.
2. Divide soybeans in soaking liquid into three equal portions.
3. Put one portion in a blender and blend at high speed for 2½ to 3 minutes, or until very smooth.
4. Pour purée into a large bowl. Repeat the second portion in the same way. Purée the remaining soybeans in the same way.
5. Rinse out blender with ¾ C water to retrieve any purée that may cling to blender's walls. Pour into the bowl.
6. Pour 5 C plus 2 T of hot water into a large cooking pot and bring to a boil. Pour all purée into boiling water from the bowl.
7. Heat over high heat about 5 to 6 minutes, then reduce heat to low. Continue cooking for 8 minutes, stirring bottom of pot with a wooden or a bamboo spatula to prevent sticking. Take care so that the pot does not boil over.
8. Set colander into a large bowl. Moisten a pressing sack made of cheesecloth or light cotton dishtowel and line colander with the sack, fitting mouth of sack around rim of colander. Pour hot purée from cooking pot. Then, transfer liquid (soymilk) into a large cooking pot.
9. Twist hot sack to close. Using a wooden spatula press sack against colander. Pour soymilk into a large pot.
10. Moisten wooden container. Using wooden container lid, press sack, pressing as much soymilk as possible or until contents of sack weigh 16⅓ oz (460 g).
11. Contents of sack are called *okara*. *Okara* recipes are given on page 58, 59, 83, 86, 87. Liquid from sack is called soymilk. Soymilk recipes are given on page 88.
12. Pour some hot water in a pot, larger than cooking pot, and place it in soymilk cooking pot. Heat soymilk to 158–167°F (70–75°C).
13. Meantime dissolve one package, or 1¼ oz (35 g) of *nigari* into 1⅔ C (or 400 ml) water. Measure ¾ C plus 2 T solidifier (or 100 ml) solution; set aside. Keep the rest in a refrigerator for later use. The solidifier solution keeps up to 2 years in a refrigerator.
14. With wooden spatula fold over surface of soymilk. Pour 3 T solidifier solution on spatula. The solution will drip into soymilk. Stir soymilk maintaining 158–167°F (70–75°C); leave for 2 minutes. Push some surface bubbles to the sides of the pot.
15. Pour another 1½ T solidifier over surface of soymilk, stir and leave for 2 minutes.
16. Pour remaining 1½ T solidifier into curdling soymilk.
17. Stir slowly with wooden spatula after curds float on clear liquid. Turn off heat; cover pot and leave for 7 to 15 minutes.
18. If curds do not float on clear liquid, add 1 T-2T solidifier solution.
19. Moisten wooden container; line bottom and sides of container with cheesecloth or thin dishtowel.
20. Ladle curds gently into the container one layer at a time. Using rubber spatula, smooth out surface of curds.
21. Fold edges of cloth neatly over curds. Place a wooden lid on top of cloth. Set a 28 oz (800 g) weight on top of lid for 15 minutes.
22. In a large bowl, fill with cold water. Remove weight from the top of container. Slowly invert container with lid.
23. Lift out container and carefully unwrap cloth. Put *tofu* under water for 30 minutes to 1 hour. Change water 2–3 times to remove excess *nigari*.
24. Store *tofu* in an airtight container with water and keep in a refrigerator. For best flavor, serve within two days.

PREPARATION

TOFU PREPARATION TIPS

Fresh *tofu* is very fragile.

It is best to use fresh *tofu* within 24 hours after it is made. If it is not to be used right away, drain out water from the original container; add cold water and seal tight. Or place *tofu* in a flat-bottomed container and fill with water and cover. Keep *tofu* in the bottom of refrigerator. *Tofu* can be kept fresh for 3 to 4 days. If kept more than 3 to 4 days, it is recommended that *tofu* be boiled in salted water for 2 to 3 minutes. Do not freeze because the texture of *tofu* will change. However, if you prefer a different texture, you may try as follows: 1. Drain water from water-packed container. 2. Wrap *tofu* in plastic sheet. 3. Keep in freezer. 4. Color turns to light umber. This way frozen *tofu* can be stored indefinitely. Before cooking dip in water and remove plastic sheet and wash well. Frozen *tofu* has tender and meaty texture and makes excellent dishes with vegetables (see page 26). To cook fresh *tofu*, do not overcook. Always add *tofu* last in cooking. Also for better cooking, drain water out before cooking. It gives a firmer and richer flavor. Keep *tofu* in refrigerator for a couple of hours or overnight. Or faster results, see illustration below.

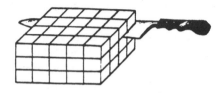

Cut *tofu* into cubes.

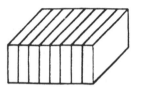

Cut *tofu* into ¹/₄ inch (0.7 cm) or ¹/₂ inch (1.5 cm) thick slices.

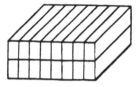

Cut *tofu* crosswise into halves; then slice into 8 pieces.

DRAINING *TOFU*

As *tofu* holds a large amount of water, sometimes it is necessary to drain or press it well before using.

A

Wrap *tofu* in gauze, place between two boards and let stand to drain.

B

Boil *tofu* briefly. Wrap in a gauze and place between two boards; let stand to drain.

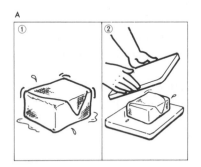

For faster results, place *tofu* on several layers of towels on cutting board and top with water-filled bowl. Change the towels often.

PREPARATION

Rice Cooking

There are two types of rice available; white short-grain rice and white long-grain rice. Use white short-grain rice for Japanese dishes. The short-grain rice is more glutinous than the long-grain rice. In the U.S., short-grain rice is grown extensively in California. Newly cropped rice needs less water and slightly shorter cooking time than old rice. A little practice is needed to make perfect rice, however if you cook a lot of rice, an automatic rice cooker will make your work a lot easier, so it's a good investment.

Rice increases in volume as it cooks, twice to three times, depending on the kind of rice you use. The following is a key to shiny and fluffy rice. Go ahead with these basic tips for successful rice cooking. It's easy.

1. Measure rice carefully.
2. Wash rice in a big bowl of water. Rub grains gently since wet grains break easily.
3. Remove any bran or polishing agent. Drain off water well. Repeat this step until water is almost clear.
4. To make fluffy and moist rice, set rice aside for at least 30 minutes in summer and one hour in winter. This allows ample time for rice to absorb water.
5. In cooking pot, add rice and correct amount of water. Cover with lid.
6. Cook rice over medium heat until water boils. Do not bring it to boiling point quickly. If the quantity of rice is large, cook rice over high heat from the beginning. The heat can be carried into the center of rice if cooked over medium heat.
7. When it begins to boil, turn heat to high and cook for 1 minute. Never lift lid while cooking.
8. Turn heat to low and cook for 4 to 5 minutes (Be careful not to overboil). Then the pot begins to steam.
9. Reduce heat to the lowest for 10 minutes.
10. Turn off the heat and let rice stand covered for 10 minutes. During these 10 minutes the grains are allowed to ''settle'', and the cooking process is completed by the heat retained in the rice and the walls of the pot.

How To Make *Sushi* Rice

Prepare a non-metallic tub, preferably wooden or glass (make sure it is not polished since the vinegar will remove the wax polish).

1. Wash mixing tub well. Dry with kitchen towel.
2. Put cooked rice into mixing tub and spread evenly over the bottom of mixing tub.
3. Sprinkle vinegar mixture generously over the rice. You may not need all of vinegar mixture. Do not add too much liquid.
4. With a large wooden spoon, mix rice with a slicing motion.
5. While you mix, fan using the other hand or an electric fan. This is not to cool *sushi* rice, but to puff the extra liquid away.
6. Keep *sushi* rice in the wooden tub, covered with a damp cloth.

Cooked Rice

COOKED RICE	Rice	Water
2^1/$_2$ C	1 C	1^1/$_4$ C
5 C	2 C	2^1/$_2$ C
7^1/$_2$ C	3 C	3^1/$_4$ C
10 C	4 C	5 C

Sushi Rice

COOKED RICE	Rice	Water	PREPARED *SUSHI* RICE	VINEGAR MIXTURE		
				Vinegar	Sugar	Salt
2^1/$_2$ C	1 C	1^1/$_5$ C	2^1/$_2$ C	2 T	^{1}/$_2$ T	1 t
5 C	2 C	2 C	5 C	3^1/$_2$ T	1 T	1^1/$_2$ t
7^1/$_2$ C	3 C	*3-3^1/$_4$ C	7^1/$_2$ C	5 T	1^1/$_2$ T	2 t
10 C	4 C	*4-4^1/$_2$ C	10 C	7 T	2 T	3t(1 T)

C=cup   T=tablespoon   t=teaspoon
* makes softer rice.
The above vinegar mixture proportions are the basic recipe.
Sugar can be increased for a sweeter taste.

PREPARATION

How To Make *Dashi* Stock

Good *dashi* stock is a key to all Japanese dishes. It enhances not only soups but any recipe. If you can master *dashi* stock making then you'll master the basic technique of Japanese cooking. There are two requirements for making *dashi* stock: Be quick and never boil the liquid.
Avoid keeping leftover *dashi* stock more than 2 or 3 days in a refrigerator. It may be frozen in an ice cube tray. However, earlier use of it recommended since longer storage will lose in flavor.

Kombu kelp stock
Makes approx 4 cups
4 C (1 qt)   water
6 in (15 cm)   length *kombu* kelp (1 1/3 oz/40 g)

Wipe kelp with a damp cloth (do not wash, or much of the flavor will be lost), soak in 4 cups of water, and let it sit for an hour. Heat to the boiling point, but remove the kelp just before the water actually boils.

Bonito stock
Makes approx 4 cups
4 C (1 qt)   water
4 in (10 cm)   square *kombu* kelp (1 oz/30 g)
1 C dried bonito flakes (1/3–1/2 oz/10–15 g)

A) *Ichiban dashi* (Primary *dashi*): Put kelp in 4 cups of water. Heat, uncovered, over medium high heat until the water reaches boiling point; remove the kelp immediately. Add 1/4 cup water and heat. Add 1 cup of dried bonito flakes just before the water reaches boiling point. When the foam begins to rise, reduce heat and simmer for 10 seconds. Turn off heat, and add a pinch of salt which will keep the water from absorbing more bonito flavor and tasting too strong. Let stand until the flakes sink to the bottom. Strain and store.

B) *Niban dashi* (Secondary *dashi*): Primary *dashi* is best for clear soups. Secondary *dashi* can be used for thick soups, cooking vegetables and many other ways as a cooking stock.
Place the kelp and bonito flakes reserved from the primary *dashi* in 4 cups water. Heat to the boiling point, reduce heat and simmer for 15 minutes. Turn off heat and strain.

Sardine stock
Makes approx 4 cups
4 C (1 qt)   water
2 T *sake*
10 dried small sardines
4 in (10 cm)   square *kombu* kelp (1 oz/30 g)

As dried small sardines produce a stock with a strong fish flavor, this stock is used mostly for *miso* soups. Remove head and intestines of 10 pieces of dried sardine. This proccess reduces bitterness and strong fish flavor from stock. After washing, soak in 4 cups of water 2 to 3 hours. Heat until the water just reaches body temperature. Strain.

Instant *dashi* stock
Makes approx 4 cups
4 C (1 qt)   water
1/3 T instant *dashi* mix (1/8 oz/4 g)

Add instant *dashi* mix to boiling water and stir until powder dissolves.
Variation: Use the liquid in which dried *shiitake* mushrooms was soaked. Add 1 teaspoon instant *dashi* mix to 1 cup water and mix with the *shiitake* soaking liquid.

COOKING TIPS

Deep Frying

Tempura is a representative "batter-fried" food in Japan. It is probably the best known Japanese dish.
Four points for successful *Tempura*
1) Fresh ingredients.
2) Good vegetable oil.
3) Constant frying temperature.
4) Lumpy batter.
Prepare all ingredients to be deep-fried ahead of time. Preferably keep in a refrigerator until last minute. Make the *tempura* batter just before the actual deep-frying. The *tempura* batter, mixture of ice water, eggs and flour, should never be stirred well. Mix lightly — batter should be lumpy. All foods should be thoroughly dried before dredging. If you prefer a thick coating to thin batter, use less ice water than the recipe.
In general, deep-frying requires a large amount of oil in the wok, heavy cast iron skillet or deep-fryer. The use of polyunsaturated vegetable oil is strongly recommended for deep-frying. None of the pure vegetable oils contains cholesterol. The right temperature for deep-frying is 330–355°F (165–180°C). The oil should reach this temperature before any ingredients are added. An easy way to tell whether the oil has reached the desired temperature is adding a drop of batter into the oil. If the drop of batter reaches the bottom and slowly returns to the surface, the oil is not yet hot enough. If the batter drops half way to the bottom and immdediately bounces up to the surface, the oil is ready for deep-frying. Drop in ingredients and deep-fry until golden. Adjust the temperature to maintain a constant frying temperature. Frying temperature of 340°F (170°C) is recommended for vegetables. Use deep-frying thermometer to maintain a constant oil temperature. Skim the surface of the oil occasionally to keep it clean. Start with vegetables and then shrimp which requires a higher temperature. The oil used for deep-frying can be saved and reused. To grant your oil longer life, remove crumbs with a fine mesh strainer. The quality of used oil is judged by its clarity, not by the number of times used nor the length of time used. Fresh oil is light in color and clear. If the used oil is still relatively clear, it is readily usable again. For the second time round, it is recommended to deep-fry chicken or meats coated with bread crumbs. To remove odor in oil, deep-fry some potatoes uncoated. The moisture in potato absorbs odor while it is deep-fried. The proportion of 3 : 1 (used oil: fresh oil) is also usable again for deep-frying meats and chicken, but not for *tempura*. To store the used oil, first strain with a fine mesh strainer while oil is still hot. Then place the oil in a heatproof container and allow to cool. Cover and store in dark and cool place or in the refrigerator.

Grilling, Broiling, Pan-frying, Baking

Apart from eating fish raw, grilling is the best preferable method. Japan has access to a variety of fish and shellfish in the seas surrounding the country. So raw fish and seafood have always been valued and appreciated and have become an integral part of diet. When they grill fish, it is served as if the fish on the plate is swimming in water. The grilling method is used to cook food quickly over very high heat so that the outside is crisp while the inside flesh remains tender and moist. The ingredients must be fresh. Grilling can be done with two different ways; direct and indirect heat. If you do charcoal grill, prepare charcoal fire in advance so that heat gets very hot. For stove top grilling, coat the rack with thin film of oil, then heat the unit before you place food on. Fish and meats are often marinated or basted with marinade sauces before and during cooking. Marinade sauces are combinations of *sake, mirin* or sugar, soy sauce and fresh ginger which has the same tenderizing enzyme as papaya and pineapple. Since everything is eaten with chopsticks, food is cut into bite-size pieces except small whole fish. This also reduces both marinating and grilling time. Grill 60% on one side and 40% on the other side. For pan-frying, heat and add a small amount of oil. Heat the oil, then tilt the skillet so the oil covers the surface. When the oil begins to form a light haze, it is ready to pan-fry the ingredients. Cook over high heat, so that fish or meat except pork is tender and moist inside and the flavor is sealed in. If longer cooking is necessary, reduce heat and cover for a few minutes. You may need to add some marinade sauce to the pan. Then remove the lid and continue to cook until all liquid evaporates. For oven baking, preheat the oven to the required temperature and place food in the center of the oven to allow for even baking. Microwave oven method is not recommended for Japanese cooking. Microwave cooking takes moisture out of fish and will not give a crispy finish. To eliminate fish odor in the kitchen after cooking, heat a small amount of soy sauce in skillet and burn. The soy sauce aroma helps to remove the fish odor.

Nabemono Cooking (one-pot dishes)

Nabemono includes any dish that is cooked in one pot and eaten on the table. Therefore it has a great many varieties besides *sukiyaki* and *shabu-shabu*, and one of the main characteristics is in the cooking stock. In *sukiyaki* you only pick up solid ingredients from the pot, while in *yosenabe* you take the broth together and enjoy it as a soup. In *shabu-shabu; mizutaki* or *chirinabe*, you take the cooked but unseasoned ingredients and dip into sauces. In *dotenabe*, the brown broth is enjoyed as a *miso*-based soup. In *oden-nabe* fish products and vegetables are stewed for a long time and eaten with the broth.
In any type of *nabemono*, you can choose any ingredients you like. Basically *nabemono* needs no special cooking technique, but there are several points: When selecting ingredients, think not only of the colors but the affinity. Avoid harsh-tasting or strong-odor or fragile food. When preparing, cut each ingredient according to its cooking time so that all ingredients are ready to eat at the same time. Some foods need parboiling. Burdock root should be parboiled and blanched in cold water. *Daikon* radish and *konnyaku* must be parboiled to remove harsh taste. Dried foods should be softened well.

Continued on page 96

COOKING TIPS

Continued from page 95

Simmering

A Japanese full course meal consists of raw fish which is *sashimi*, a broiled or grilled food and a simmered food. So, simmered food plays an important role in the Japanese kitchen.

Simmering food requires special preparation
1) Simmering liquid is generally made of primary *dashi*, or *ichiban-dashi* seasoned with *sake*, *mirin* or sugar, salt, soy sauce and/or *miso*. *Sake* and *mirin* are often used in Japanese cooking. They are mild in taste and add zest to the food.
2) You may need some special cutting techniques for vegetables such as diagonal slices, flower-cuts, trimming to enhance the appearance of the finished dish.
3) Some ingredients need parboiling to remove harsh or bitter taste and rawness. Also, some ingredients take longer to cook. These ingredients are sometimes pre-cooked in different pans, then added to the simmering liquid. Simmered food can be served as a single dish or as one-pot dish. The ingredients and simmering liquid for the one-pot dishes are prepared ahead of time and arranged attractively on large platters.

The size of the pot is determined by the amount of ingredients to be cooked. For simmering whole fish or fish fillets, use wide flat-bottomed pan. A thick-bottomed pot will distribute the heat more evenly. If simmering for longer time, use a deep pot that holds an ample amount of simmering liquid. Slow electric cooker will do the same effect.

Indispensable for simmering is a drop lid which is a light-weight wooden lid slightly smaller than the pot. It is made of well-dried cypress or cedar. It is placed directly on top of the food to keep it immersed in the liquid, enabling the flavors to be absorbed. Wood is likely to absorb the liquid in the pot and many odors, so always soak the drop-lid in water for a few minutes before using. Heat-proof flat plate, aluminum foil and heavy butcher-paper are good substitutes for wooden lid. Skim off occasionally. Use light seasoning for simmering liquid. The less the better. You can always add more later. In general add sugar or *mirin* first, then salt, rice vinegar (if recipe calls for) and soy sauce. Remember to control simmering temperature so that the liquid can be slowly absorbed into the ingredients.

Steaming

Steaming is one of the best way of retaining more nutrients and natural flavor than other conventional means of cooking. Steaming seals in the natural juices of meats and vegetables which are delicious when served over rice. There are many different types of steamers. Wok with a cover will work as a good steamer. Multitiered bamboo steamers may be purchased. However, a large pot with a cover will suffice for the purpose of steaming food. Steaming racks are necessary to support and elevate the plate or bowl which holds food steamed in a wok. A round cake rack will do just as well as commercially available steaming racks. You may improvise water chestnut cans with both ends removed. The rack should be put in the center of the wok or pan.

All steamers operate according to the same basic principle. The efficient circulation of steam is of paramount importance. Bamboo steamers have several tiers in which many dishes can be steamed simultaneously. The tiers and cover are set on top of a wok containing boiling water. There are also metal steamers consisting of a pot to hold the water, usually two tiers and a cover. For example, the bottom pot cooks soup stock while the two tiers are used to steam two other separate dishes. In this manner, many dishes may be steamed at once saving time and energy.

Follow the steps below for effective steaming
1) Pour water into the wok or pot so that the water level stands one inch below the steaming rack or dish of food.
2) Cover the wok and bring the water to a full boil.
3) Use only heatproof dishes for steaming.
4) Place the dish of food atop the steaming rack. Cover and bring to the boiling point again. Turn the temperature down to medium high and allow to steam for the specified time.
5) Check the water level when longer steaming is necessary.

Stir frying, Sautéeing

This cooking method combines the elements of high heat and constant tossing to seal in the flavor and juices of meat and vegetables. Thus, this technique is often used for Chinese cooking. Stir-frying cooks protein foods thoroughly at the same time leaving them tender and juicy. Vegetables retain their natural color and crisp texture when stir fried. It is important that slices are uniform in size so that they can be cooked evenly. Some vegetables may need parboiling before stir-frying. Prepare all neccessary seasonings before stir-frying. Heat the wok or skillet until it barely gets hot and add a small amount of oil (usually 2 T), then roll the oil around to cover the surface of the wok. When the oil begins to form a light haze, add the ingredients. Follow the recipe and remember to adjust the temperature control at the proper stir-frying temperature. Actual stir-frying involves vigorous arm action in the constant stirring and tossing of the food. Serve immediately while still hot.

UTENSILS

BAMBOO MAT (MAKISU), BAMBOO STEAMER ────── It is made of narrow strips of bamboo bound with strong cotton yarns. Bamboo mat is used for rolling up or draining ingredients.

BAMBOO SKEWERS ────── For Japanese cooking, bamboo skewers are a very handy tool. They are not only used for many grilled dishes, but to test foods for doneness by pricking and also for cooking raw shrimp to prevent curling while boiling.
Moisten bamboo skewers before skewering for grilling to prevent breaking or burning.

CHOPSTICKS (HASHI)

How To Use Chopsticks
1. Chopsticks are placed on the chopstick rest thinner ends on your left. Hold the center with your right fingers.
2. Pick up and add left fingers beneath. Immediately slide your right fingers towards right ends.
3. Now hold steady, the upper stick between thumb and forefinger, the lower stick between the tip of third finger and the base of thumb, with middle finger lifting the upper stick.
4. Release left fingers. Fix the lower stick and move the upper stick up and down using forefinger and middle finger.

DROP LID ────── This is a lightweight wooden lid slightly smaller than the circumference of the cooking pot. In cooking simmered dishes, it is placed directly on top of the ingredients to keep them immersed in the liquid, enabling the flavors to be absorbed.
Always soak the drop-lid in water for a few minutes before using. It absorbs the liquid in the pot and may carry odor. Aluminum foil or heavey butcher-paper is a good substitute for a wooden lid if you can't obtain one. Cut out a circle a little bigger than the pot. A wooden lid can press down the liquid, but paper may go up and part from it, so fold it up against the sides of the pot.

EARTHEN POTS ────── Earthen pots conduct heat gently but maitain it well, which is a great advantage in *nabemono* cooking. Despite the heavy appearance, earthen pots are very fragile. To prevent cracks, fill with heavily salted hot water and heat until the water decreases. Do not discard the water and allow to cool. Pour in hot water again and heat to boiling. This will make the pot durable for long time use.
When placing over heat, be sure to wipe off moisture from outside bottom and start with low heat. Do not put hot earthen pot into cold water.
If cracks appear, cook rice gruel in it and cracks will be sealed. If the bottom is burnt, do not scrub but pour in vinegar and water; heat for 10 minutes and then scrub. Wash after it is cooled, dry thoroughly and store in a dry place.

JAPANESE GRINDING BOWL ────── Pottery bowl serrated on the inside. It is useful when grinding small amount of food such as sesame seeds, or *miso* (soybean paste). If using newly bought one, grind vegetable scraps to remove pottery powder between the grooves and to smooth the surface. After each use, wash with a brush, scrubbing along the grooves. Use a bamboo skewer to remove tiny bits. Wipe off moisture and dry. When storing, do not place other ware on top to prevent abrasion.

SKIMMER ────── Fine netted stainless ladle to skim off splashes of batter while cooking *tempura*. It can be used to take *tempura* out. Other than *tempura*, use it to skim off residue or as a strainer. It easily gets greasy, so wash carefully using a brush.

WOODEN PESTLES ────── Used to grind food in a grinding bowl. Choose one of firm wood such as Japanese pepper tree, and twice as long as the bowl diameter. Prior to use, soak in water and pat dry. This is to prevent sticking. After use, wash thoroughly and dry well.

WOK ────── A wok has many advantages for deep frying, stir frying, sautéeing and steaming. Because of its large surface area with food moving quickly, the rounded bottom requires a minimum amount of oil, and the slanted sides protect against splattering. To give the wok stability, place the adapter ring over the largest burner, with the side slanting upwards to allow the center of the wok closer proximity to the burner. A newly purchased wok should be given special seasoning. First fill wok 3/4 full with water; heat until lukewarm. Add detergent and scrub well with a brush. Repeat. Cut up half an onion into slices. Heat 2 t oil in the wok until hot over high heat. Add onion slices and stir fry rotating wok constantly to coat sloping sides until onion slices are almost burnt to black. Discard the onion and oil. Wash the wok with hot water and dry. Whenever the wok is used for steaming, it must be reseasoned afterward in order to prevent food from sticking. The cover and steaming rack are for steaming food. A steaming rack made of metal is used to elevate plates of food above the boiling water in wok while steaming. Special Japanese steamers are available, but unless a lot of food is steamed, a wok with steaming rack and cover is sufficient.

INGREDIENTS

ATSUAGE (deep-fried *tofu* cutlet)·*ABURAAGE* (deep-fried *tofu* pouch) ——— *Atsuage* is a deep-fried regular *tofu*. It is fried until the outside becomes crisp and golden brown but the inside is still white. *Aburaage* is also deep-fried *tofu*, but before frying it is cut into thin sheets.

BAMBOO SHOOTS ——— Bamboo shoots are one of the most common ingredients in Asian cooking. In Japan, bamboo shoots are "cooked-fresh", canned in water and available all the year round. Occasionally, such water-packed bamboo is exported and available in U.S..

BEAN THREADS ——— These are long, dry noodles made of mung bean flour. They keep on the shelf indefinitely. Soak them in warm water for 15 minutes before use. They may also be deep fried in hot oil. Do not soak them in water prior to deep frying though. Use them as a noodle in soups, or with stir-fried vegetables and meat. To keep them as clean as possible place them in a large paper bag before removing wrapper. Break off the amount needed and store remainder in a bag.

CHINESE CABBAGE (bok choy) ——— This versatile, greenish-white leafed cabbage is used in stir fry and one-pot dishes. It is also added to soups, and made into pickles. A heavy, succulent vegetable, Chinese caggage is often found in supermarkets, not to mention in Oriental food stores. It is also known as "celery cabbage" and "*nappa* (sometimes '*Napa*') cabbage". Avoid produce with spotted leaves, if possible. Store the same as you would lettuce.

CHINESE MUSTARD, DRIED ——— Pungent powder. Mix 1 tablespoon dry powder to 1 tablespoon water for average proportion. Store dry powder on shelf indefinitely.

CLOUD EARS ——— See page 101.

DAIKON RADISH ——— *Daikon* radish is rich in vitamins, and its leaves contain much calcium. This radish is thought to aid digestion of oily foods. It is good for simmered dishes.

DASHI STOCK ——— See page 94.

DRIED BONITO ——— This is an important ingredient in *dashi* stock. A stick of dried bonito looks like a 6–8 in (15–20cm) long brownish hunk of wood.
Shaved, dried bonito flakes are also available in packs and convenient to use.
Dried bonito "thread" shavings are often used as a garnish. Such "thread" shavings look like rosy-beige excelsior and have a pleasant flavor. If you cannot obtain them, use regular dried bonito flakes.

DRIED GOURD STRIPS (*kampyo*) ——— See page 101.

EGGPLANTS ——— Eggplants used here are the 6 in (15cm) variety that weigh approximately 10 oz (285g) each, rather than the small Japanese eggplants that are on the average 4 in (10cm) long and weigh 2–3 oz (60–90g) each. Because size varies with region and season, weights are included to offer a guideline. If using the small Japanese variety, substitute 3–4 eggplants in these recipes.

ENOKITAKE MUSHROOMS ——— *Enokitake* mushrooms are mild-flavored and have a pleasant crispness and aroma. They are often used in soups. There are canned *enokitake* mushrooms but fresh ones are better.

GANMODOKI (deep-fried *tofu* burgurs) ——— *Ganmodoki* consists of crumbled *tofu*, sesame seeds, ginkgo nuts and slivered vegetables like carrots, mushrooms, and burdock bound together with grated mountain yam. This *tofu*-based mixture is formed into 3 in (8cm) patties or 1 1/2 in (4cm) balls, then deep fried. They are used in simmered dishes. They go well with soy sauce. See page 52.

GINGERROOT ——— Ginger is a pungent, aromatic rootstalk of a genus Zingiber, tropical Asiatic and Polinesian herb. It is a popular spice all over the world.
The pungent substance promotes both appetite and digestion.
When using for stir-fried dishes, shred and cook in hot oil to extract the aroma. In this oil cook the other ingredients. Choose fresh root without wrinkles.

GRILLED *TOFU* (*yaki-dofu*) ——— Grilled *tofu* is grilled on both sides over charcoal, thus producing its firm texture. It is easy to recognize by the light mottling on the skin. If *yaki-dofu* is not available, you can make it easily. Drain regular *tofu* and lightly grill each side of *tofu* over high heat. Grilled *tofu* is often used in boiled dishes such as *Sukiyaki*.

HOISIN SAUCE ——— Pungent, sweet condiment sauce made of soybeans, spices, chili and sugar. Once opened, store in a jar with tight lid. Keeps refrigerated for about 6 months.

INGREDIENTS

HOT BEAN PASTE (chili paste with soybeans) ——— Soybean sauce made from soybeans, chili peppers and sometimes garlic. Comes in cans or jars. Refrigerated, keeps indefinitely in tightly sealed jars. Degree of hotness may vary between different brands.

JAPANESE CUCUMBER ——— Recipes in this book call for American cucumbers, which are equivalent to 2 or 3 Japanese cucumbers. In general, peel and seed cucumbers unless skin is delicate and thin and seeds are immature. If using the Japanese variety, it is not necessary to peel or seed. However to smooth the rough surface and to bring out the skin color, dredge the cucumber in salt and roll it back and forth on a cutting board using the palm of your hand. Wash well.

JAPANESE HOT PEPPER ——— Red pepper is used fresh or dried. Dried and ground coarse pepper is called *ichimi*, or one flavor spice. This *ichimi* is one of the component ingredients of *shichimi* or 7-spice mixture. *Shichimi* is a collection of seven dried and ground flavors: red pepper flakes (*togarashi*); roughly ground, brown *sansho* pepper pods; minute flakes of dried mandarin orange peel; dark green *nori* seaweed bits; black hemp seeds; white poppy seeds; and black sesame seeds.

KAMABOKO·CHIKUWA (steamed fish paste) ——— *Kamaboko* is made mainly from fish protein. Good *kamaboko* is white and elastic and the cut end is glossy. Keep in refrigerator. *Chikuwa* literally means ring of bamboo. Both *kamaboko* and *chikuwa* go well with horseradish soy sauce.

KOMBU (kelp) ——— *Kombu* is one of the basic ingredients used for making *dashi* stock. When you use it, never wash or rinse. The speckled surface of the kelp holds flavor, so do not wash. Kelp contains the most iodine of all seaweeds.

KONNYAKU·ITO-KONNYAKU ——— *Konnyaku* made from the roots of "devil's tongue" has no calories. It must be simmerd for a long time before eating. *Ito-konnyaku* is *konnyaku* strips.

KOYA-DOFU (freeze-dried *tofu* or frozen *tofu*) ——— This is made from soybeans. One package usually contains five to six pieces. It looks like a beige sponge and is very light. Prior to cooking, it should be soaked in lukewarm water until soft. It will double the volume. It is easily simmered and it goes well with soy sauce. Freeze-dried *tofu* was originally a daily food for monks in Japan. Now it is popular with everyone.

LOTUS ROOT ——— The flesh is white and "crunchy". Long tubular hollows run through the entire length of the root. When preparing lotus root for cooking, pare it first. Then cut into rounds. The shape should be attractive. To prevent discoloring it should be immersed for a short time in a mixture of alum and water or vinegar and water. This also gets rid of any hashness in flavor. It can then be boiled in water containing a little vinegar. It goes well with vinegared dishes.

MIRIN ——— *Mirin* is heavily sweetened *sake*, used for cooking. *Mirin* is called "sweet cooking rice wine". *Sake* sweetened with sugar can be substituted.

MISO ——— *Miso* is fermented soybean paste. The colors range from yellow to brown; yellow *miso* is referred to as white *miso* in this book. Brown *miso* is called red *miso*. Since there are various kinds of *miso*, it might be helpful to learn about *miso* by buying small quantities of various kinds. It is used for soups, dressings, sauces, etc.

NATTO (fermented soybeans) ——— This is a fermented soybeans preparation made by the action of special bacteria. It has a rich cheese-like aroma and flavor and is sticky. With good *natto*, the sticky "threads" formed while mixing shoud be strong and stubborn and the beans should be moderately moist.

NIGARI (solidifier) ——— Crystalized salts are made from clean sea water by natural evaporation. The salts are placed on a strainer to catch liquid. The liquid from the salts is *nigari*.
Natural *nigari* contains 20% of magnesium chloride, 6% of calcium chloride, some minerals and mostly sodium. *Nigari* is available from local *tofu* shops, natural food stores, some chemical supply houses through mail orders or some special food markets in Japan. However, natural *nigari* is no longer available today in Japan. Because salt making process has been changed since 1971. Japan imports natural *nigari* from China and refines it to make powder for commercial use.
In the West, Epsom salts, lemon, lime juice or vinegar is generally used as solidifiers. A taste of *tofu* depends on the type of *nigari* you use.

NORI SEAWEED ——— The best quality *nori* seaweed is glossy black-purple. It is used after toasting which

Continued on page 100

improves flavor and texture. *Nori* seaweed grows around bamboo stakes placed underwater. When the time comes, it is gathered, washed, laid in thin sheets and dried. It contains lots of protein.

OKARA ——— *Okara* is a by-product of the *tofu*-making process. It looks like moist, white, crumbly saw dust. It is a delight to make various dishes with this high-protein, low-calorie food *okara.*

OYSTER SAUCE ——— Thick brown sauce made from oysters and soy sauce. Used to enhance flavor or as a dip. Keeps indefinitely in the refrigerater.

PANKO (dehydrated bread crumbs) ——— Japanese dehydrated bread crumbs with a coarser texure than regular bread crumbs are available at most supermarkets or Oriental groceries.

SAKE ——— *Sake* is made by inoculating steamed mold (*koji*) and then allowing fermentation to occur. It is then refined. In Japan, *sake* is the most popular beverage but it is also used in various ways in cooking.

SANSHO, KINOME SPRIGS ——— Both the leaves and seed pods of *sansho* are used. Dried leaves are powdered and used as a spice, *sansho* pepper. The young leaves called *kinome* sprigs are mainly used to garnish foods.

SESAME OIL ——— Made from sesame seeds which are rich in oil and protein. This oil has a unique taste and aroma. It is mixed with salad oil and used for frying *tempura* or used to add flavor and aroma to the dressing used on Japanese-style *aemono* dishes.

SESAME SEEDS ——— Both black and white sesame seeds are used in Japanese cooking. When toasted, sesame seeds have a much richer flavor. Still richer, however, are ground sesame seeds. To grind sesame seeds use a *suribachi* (Japanese grinding bowl). Before grinding, toast seeds in a dry frying pan. It is a nice garnish.

SHICHIMI–TOGARASHI (7-spice powder) ——— This is a good spice for sprinkling over *udon, soba, mizutaki,* etc. Because it loses its aroma quickly, buy it in small quantities and store, tightly covered. See JAPANESE HOT PEPPER section.

SHIITAKE MUSHROOMS ——— Both fresh and dried *shiitake* mushrooms can be obtained. Dried ones should be soaked in water before using. This soaking water makes *dashi* stock (Japanese soup stock). Fresh *shiitake* mushrooms have a distinctive, appealing "woody-fruity" flavor. *Shiitake* mushrooms are good for simmered dishes because of their special flavor. The best one has thick, brown velvety cap and firm flesh.

SHISO LEAVES ——— These minty, aromatic leaves come in green and red varieties. The red type is used to make *umeboshi* (pickled plum).

SHIMEJI MUSHROOMS ——— Fresh *shimeji* mushrooms should be delicately crisp. The stems should be short and plump, and the flesh should be white. White mushrooms will do as substitute if *shimeji* mushrooms are not available.

SOYBEANS ——— Soybeans were one of the "five sacred grains" of ancient China. They have many cultivars including black and yellow ones and countless uses: they can be used in stews, turned into soy paste, soymilk, also *tofu*, and can be used as a meat substitute.

SOY SAUCE ——— Soy sauce is made from soybeans and salt. It is the primary seasoning of Japanese cooking. It is used for simmered foods, dressings, soups; many kinds of Japanese dishes. Ordinary soy sauce is dark, but one which has a light color is also available. The light soy sauce does not darken the colors of food, and it is salty enough. Thick soy sauce is a good seasoning for raw fish, *sashimi*. It is rather sweet.

TOFU ——— *Tofu*, "bean curd" in English, is an important product of soybeans. It is rich in proteins, vitamins, calcium, and minerals. It is low in calories and saturated fats, and entirely free of cholesterol. There are two kinds of *tofu*; firm *tofu* and soft *tofu*.

TREFOIL (*mitsuba*) ——— Trefoil is a member of the parsley family. The flavor is somewhere between sorrel and celery. It accents the flavor of many Japanese dishes.

UMEBOSHI ——— *Umeboshi* are made every June when green plums come onto the market in Japan. Green, unripe plums are soaked in brine, packed with red *shiso* leaves and left to mature in the salty bath. In Japan *umeboshi* have long been regarded as a tonic. Not only are they thought to help in digestion, but they also keep the intestinal tract clean. This may be one of the reasons why *umeboshi* are served with the traditional Japanese breakfast. Also *umeboshi* paste can be a seasoning.

INGREDIENTS

VINEGAR ——— Japanese rice vinegar is milder than most Western vinegars. Lightness and relative sweetness are characteristics of rice vinegar. Use cider vinegar rather than anything synthetic if substituting.

VINEGARED FRESH GINGER

5-6 stalks young fresh ginger

Vinegar Mixture: $^1/_2$ C rice vinegar   2 T sugar   1 t salt $^1/_2$ C water

Bring vinegar mixture to a boil. Cool. Pour mixture into a glass. Cut leaves of fresh ginger, leaving about 9 in (23 cm) of stem. Clean roots. Dip only the roots into boiling salted water. Remove immediately. Shake off water. Dip in vinegar mixture while hot.

WASABI ——— *Wasabi* is Japanese horseradish. It is pale green in color. It has a more delicate aroma and is milder tasting than Western horseradish. In Japan both fresh and powdered *wasabi* are available, but it is hard to obtain fresh *wasabi* in other countries. The edible part of *wasabi* is the root. Usually it comes in a powdered form or in a tube, but the fragrance of fresh *wasabi* is much richer than powdered *wasabi*. The powder should be mixed with water to make a thick paste. *Wasabi* accompanies most raw fish dishes, and also *Sushi*. Raw fish may be hard to try for the first time, but with the added taste of soy sauce and *wasabi*, it will become one of your favorites.

YUZU CITRON ——— Japanese citron. The fragrant rind is grated and added as a garnish to soups and other dishes. This citrus fruit appears also in Chinese and Korean cooking. In the West where *yuzu* citron is not often available, lemon or lime rind or zest can be used though neither is quite the same.

YUBA (bean curd sheets) ——— Dried soybean curd packaged in rolls or in flat sheets. It is made from soymilk which is gently heated in a special pot, a thin film covers its surface. The film is called *yuba* and is lifted off by fine bamboo sticks and dried over a charcol fire. The color is creamy white, sometimes dyed in yellow. They tear more easily and become somewhat brittle when dried. The commonly-sold dried *yuba* is available at Oriental markets. See page 102 on nuturients. Sometimes fresh one is available. The fresh *yuba* has fine fragrant richness and is considered a true delicacy.

YAM NOODLE (*shirataki*) ——— Thin transparent gelatin-like noodles, similar to bean threads. It is made from devil's tongue root, has no calories. *Konnyaku* (see page 99) made from the same root.

How To Soften Dried Foods

Dried *shiitake* mushrooms

Dried mushrooms must be soaked in warm water until soft, which takes about 1 hour. Place a flat pan lid, drop-lid, or any similar object on mushrooms to keep them submerged. Filling a bowl to the brim with water, adding mushrooms, or laying a plate (that has enough area to keep mushrooms submerged) on top works just as well. Mushrooms soften quicker in warm water than in cold, and a drop-lid not only keeps mushrooms immersed but also prevents water from cooling off, which would slow the softening process. Discard stems and use only caps. Soaking liquid makes a good stock.

Dried bean threads

Another kind of gelatin noodle. This kind is easier to handle because it does not lose shape when cooked. To soften, soak in warm water until the center becomes transparent; drain.

Dried cloud ears (*kikurage*)

Black mushrooms which grow on mulberry trees. Look for well-dried whole mushrooms. Soak in water for 10 to 20 minutes until widely spread. Use luke warm water when in a hurry. Wash carefully and remove roots. They swell about 5 times after softening.

Dried gourd strips (*kampyo*)

Gourd is peeled thinly into long strips and dried well. Look for a flexible one in milky white color, with sweet fragrance, and of even width.

To soften rub well in water and squeeze lightly. Sprinkle with generous amount of salt and rub well with fingers. Rinse off salt and cook briefly in boiling water. When tender, drain in a colander and allow to cool.

Freeze-dried *tofu* (*koya dofu*)

Soak in warm water (about 140°F/60°C). Place a light lid on top to keep *tofu* under water. When completely softened, transfer into fresh water and press out opaque water several times. Squeeze out well.

Dried *wakame* seaweed

Dried *wakame* seaweed increases its volume to 3–4 times when reconstituted. Cover with abundant water until the 'flesh' becomes thicker and flexible. Over-soaking will damage the texture. To draw out a fresh green color, blanch in boiling water and rinse in cold water at once. This method will also remove the odor.

Dried small shrimp

Soak in warm water for about 30 minutes to soften before use. Keeps on shelf indefinitely in a covered jar.

Composition of Nutrients in 100 grams (3½ ounces) of Beef, Eggs, Milk, Tofu & Soybean Products

Types of Food	Food Energy (kcal)	Moisture (g)	Protein (g)	Fat (g)	Sugar (g)	Fiber (g)	Ash (g)	Calcium (mg)	Phosphorus (mg)	Iron (mg)	Sodium (mg)	Vitamin A (I.U.)	Vitamin B₁ (mg)	Vitamin B₂ (mg)	Cholesterol (mg)
Beef	198	66.1	20.4	12.1	0.5	0	0.9	4	140	2.9	50	20	0.11	0.3	83
Eggs	158	74.7	12.3	11.2	0.9	0	0.9	55	200	1.8	130	640	0.08	0.48	428
Milk	58	88.7	2.9	3.2	4.5	0	0.7	100	90	0.1	50	110	0.03	0.15	11
Soybeans	396	12.5	35.3	19.0	23.7	4.5	5.0	240	580	9.4	1	0	0.83	0.30	0
Soymilk	65	87.9	3.2	3.6	4.8	0	0.5	31	44	1.2	50	0	0.07	0.02	0
Soft *Tofu*	58	89.4	5.0	3.3	1.7	0	0.6	90	65	1.1	4	0	0	0.10	0
Firm *Tofu*	77	86.8	6.8	5.0	0.8	0	0.6	120	85	1.4	3	0	0	0.07	0
Grilled *Tofu*	88	84.8	7.8	5.7	1.0	0	0.7	150	110	1.6	4	0	0	0.07	0
Deep-fried *Tofu* Cutlets	151	75.9	10.7	11.3	1.0	0.1	1.1	240	150	2.6	3	0	0	0.07	0
Deep-fried *Tofu* Pouches	388	44.0	18.6	33.1	2.8	0.1	1.4	300	230	4.2	10	0	0	0.06	0
Deep-fried *Tofu* Burgers	233	63.5	15.3	17.8	1.9	0.2	1.4	270	200	3.6	190	0	0	0.03	0
Freeze-dried *Tofu*	533	8.1	50.2	33.4	5.3	0	2.8	590	710	9.4	8	12	0	0.02	0
Dried bean curd (*Yuba*)	511	6.5	53.2	28.0	8.9	0	3.4	200	600	8.1	13	20	0.20	0.08	0
Okara	89	81.1	4.8	3.6	6.4	3.3	0.8	100	65	1.2	4	0	0.11	0.04	0
Fermented Soybeans (*Natto*)	200	59.5	16.5	10.0	9.8	2.3	1.9	90	190	3.3	2	0	0.07	0.56	0
Miso	207	44.9	17.2	10.5	11.3	3.2	12.9	150	250	6.8	4300	0	0.04	0.12	0

NOTE: 3½ oz (100 g) of soybeans contain 20 mg of vitamin E.

Source: Standard Tables of Food Composition (1987) by Japanese Scientific Research Council

INDEX

NISHIMOTO TRADING CO., LTD.

IMPORTERS AND EXPORTERS

HEAD OFFICE: 2-11 KAIGAN-DORI 3-CHOME, CHUO-KU, KOBE, 650 JAPAN
TEL: (078) 391-6911~9 TLX: 5623820 NTC KB J FAX: (078) 391-1058

TOKYO OFFICE: 2-14 SOTOKANDA 3-CHOME, CHIYODAKU, TOKYO, 101
JAPAN TEL: (03) 253-5220~6 TLX: 2225504 NTC TK J FAX: (03)
257-1698

NAHA OFFICE: 1-9, MATSUYAMA 1-CHOME, NAHA, OKINAWA, 900 JAPAN
TEL: (0988) 66-1136~8 FAX: (0988) 66-6212

NEW YORK OFFICE: 21-23 EMPIRE BLVD. SOUTH HACKENSACK. N.J. 07606
TEL: (201) 641-4300 (212) 349-0056 TLX: 126663 NISHIMOTO J CTY FAX:
(0011) (201) 646-9450

LOS ANGELS OFFICE: 1111 MATEO STREET LOS ANGELES, CALIF. 90021
TEL: (213) 689-9330 TLX: 674000 NISHIMOTO LSA FAX: (0011) (213)
629-3512

SAN FRANCISCO OFFICE: 410 EAST GRAND AVENUE. SOUTH SAN
FRANCISCO, CALIF. 94080 TEL: (415) 871-2490 TLX: 278037 NISHI UR
FAX: (0011) (415) 588-5838

HONOLULU OFFICE: 537 KAAHHI STREET, HONOLULU, HAWAII 96817
TEL: (808) 847-1354 (808) 848-0761 TLX: 8478 NTC HR FAX: (0011) (808)
841-3853

DUSSELDORF OFFICE: BEETHOVENSTR 19, 4000 DUSSELDORF 1, WEST
GERMANY TEL: (0211) 660884 TLX: 8586453 NTCD D